BUILDING A
LOG HOME
FROM
SCRATCH OR KIT

BY DAN RAMSEY

TAB BOOKS Inc.
BLUE RIDGE SUMMIT, PA. 17214

FIRST EDITION

FOURTH PRINTING

Printed in the United States of America

Reproduction or publication of the content in any manner, without express per-
mission of the publisher, is prohibited. No liability is assumed with respect to
the use of the information herein.

Library of Congress Cataloging in Publication Data

Ramsey, Dan, 1945-
    Building a log home from scratch or kit.

    Includes index.
    1. Log cabins—Design and construction.   I. Title.
TH4840.R35   1983   690'.81   82-19372
ISBN 0-8306-0458-8
ISBN 0-8306-1458-3 (pbk.)

Front cover by Albert T. Cozzi.

Contents

Introduction

America is moving back to the country.

Again this year, thousands of urban families are declaring their independence and returning to the simpler life of a century ago. And they're taking some of today's technology with them: solar generators, organic farming, ultra-efficient wood stoves, and modern log homes.

The log house is a 19th century symbol of the self-made American determinedly hacking a new life out of ancient forests with his own hands. Although the modern man is no longer a "hacker" by nature, his spirit often is. Combining this spirit with that of his technological side, man has bred the log home kit and relearned the nearly lost skills of building a log shelter from scratch.

That's what this book is all about: learning the *what, why,* and *how* of returning to rustic America in a log home. Whether you're from the back woods of Connecticut or the back streets of Chicago, you'll discover how to design, build, and maintain your own home of logs. You'll learn how to prepare your own logs or buy your home in kit form, how to design the perfect log home, how to estimate construction costs, how to select and plan your building site, how to select the materials you'll need and hire labor, how to prepare the building site and—most importantly—how to build your own log home step by step. Simple instructions are offered for building log walls, installing windows and doors, rafters and trusses, roofing and finish. It's all in this book.

There's also a complete glossary of common log home construction terms you'll soon hear and use and a comprehensive listing of log home kit manufacturers.

This is truly the *complete* log home construction guide.

This book is not a singular effort. Many people contributed to its completeness and should be recognized. In random order, I'd like to acknowledge the contributions of Irene Foster of The Stimpson Associates for Justus Homes; E.P. Fillion, President of Authentic Homes Corp.; Richard A. Horn, Sales Manager of Northeastern Log Homes, Inc.; Wilbert Bossie, Director of Marketing for Ward Cabin Co., Inc.; Bob Arnold of The Alexander Company for Lincoln Logs Ltd. (NY); Janet Hubbard, Corporate Secretary of Pan Abode Cedar Homes; Nancy Selig of David Green Associates for New England Log Homes, Inc. (NELHI); Brian E. Carlisle, Manager of Northern Products Log Homes, Inc.; Steven Doctrow of Young & Rubicam for Rocky Mountain Log Homes; Don Hollenbaugh, Regional Distributor for Lincoln Log Homes, Inc. (NC); William A. Sitler, Sales Manager of Beaver Log Homes; Richard L. Wilkins, Director of Marketing for Traditional Management Co., Inc.; Lance Collister, General Manager of Real Log Homes, Inc., Montana; Richard Considine, President of Lincoln Logs, Ltd. (NY); R.L. Thuerbach, Vice President of Alpine Log Homes, Inc.; R. Dale Garrett, General Manager of Building Logs, Inc.; Bill White, Sales Manager for Lodge Logs; Bill Clark, Operation Manager of Lincoln Log Homes, Inc. (NC); Tod H. Schweizer, President of Vermont Log Buildings, Inc.; Alan S. Wilder, President of Green Mountain Cabins, Inc; John Kupferer of the Log Home Council, National Association of Home Manufacturers; James R. List, General Manager of National Log Construction Co., Inc.; Paul Maxon, President of Wilderness Log Homes; and the American Wood Council.

I also acknowledge the God who gives us trees and land and people with whom to share life. This book is dedicated to the family He thoughtfully gave me: Judy, Brendon, Byron, and Heather.

Chapter 1

The Reality of Log Homes

Abe Lincoln would be pleased.

The small hand-hewn log cabins of a century ago have evolved into massive energy-efficient log homes. Yesterday's log cabin had a wood foundation, one room, and a path. Today's log home includes as many as five bedrooms, three baths, passive solar heating, and a double garage. The modern log home reflects the expanded freedom and broadened dreams that Lincoln endeavored to build.

It's estimated that over 100,000 families now live in log homes—more than 70 percent of them full-time. Interest grows as more and more homeowners learn that they can build a log home for about the same price as a similar frame home and that they can cut costs further by doing some or all of the building themselves. That's why over 20,000 log home kits are sold each year, and thousands more are built from scratch.

Like so many other American traditions, the log home is actually an "immigrant." The log cabin was introduced to America in 1638 by the Swedish colonists of the Delaware River Valley. They brought it from northern Europe, where it had been popular for centuries. The Swedes found the New World clustered with trees and soon began cutting them down for housing. A few of their homes are still standing nearly 350 years later.

The growth of log homes in America followed the availability of trees. The settling of Kentucky, Tennessee, Ohio, Illinois, and other early territories depended on the availability of trees for simple, low-cost homes. As the settlers journeyed across the

Fig. 1-1. Many pioneer log homes still stand after a century of service (courtesy New England Log Homes, Inc.).

Plains, the trees vanished and homesteads were built around sod homes. Progress soon crossed the Rockies where the trees reappeared, giving settlers the building blocks they needed to house themselves against nature and man.

The election of William Henry Harrison as President in 1840 did much to develop the image of the "log cabin" as the birthplace of simplicity and freedom, as Harrison contrasted his log-cabin background with the estate-bred life of Martin Van Buren. Some felt he would have been warmer and safer if he had remained in his log cabin, as he caught pneumonia during the inauguration and died after only one month in office. By that time, Abraham Lincoln and Ulysses Simpson Grant had been born in log cabins to carry on the ideal.

With the advancing technology of the Industrial Revolution, the log gave way to sawmill lumber as the primary building material. It was easier to transport, easier to use, and more homogenous than logs. Dimensional lumber became the new component of housing. Log cabins were only built by hermits and North Woods trappers.

Fig. 1-2. Log homes combine the pioneer spirit and modern technology (courtesy Real Log Homes, Inc.).

Then something happened to the economy—the Great Depression. Suddenly, labor was plentiful and cheap, and the government was called on to put people to work. Many were employed to develop and enlarge national parks. Money wasn't available for building materials, so the government returned to efficiency and used available trees to build log buildings and pavilions in nearly every state with a forest. The number of log structures multiplied. World War II put the laborers back to work, and this effectively halted the proliferation of log structures for three decades.

The 1950s and '60s brought prosperity and growth to a nation

Fig. 1-3. Some log homes have walls built with milled timbers (courtesy Justus Homes).

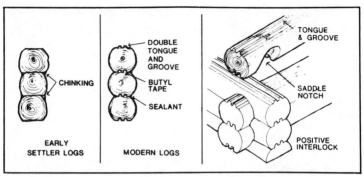

Fig. 1-4. Hand-hewed and milled logs (courtesy Beaver Log Homes).

that had tightened its belt for a long generation. Homes of dimensional lumber began sprouting up like rows in a garden and filling just as quickly. The children of this prosperity grew to adulthood in conformity. In rebellion, many of them became the "flower children" of the 1970s who searched for individuality and self-sufficiency. It was a natural move to return to log homes and do-it-yourself housing. The log home got a small but new start.

Seeing the renewed interest in log structures—and a chance for profits—a new industry was formed to supply the raw materials for log homes to do-it-yourselfers. By improving the log home through energy efficiency and new housing technology, the industry has made a "better mouse trap" which has become accepted by the middle and upper class homeowner. The 1980s promise to be a growth period for log homes built from both kits and raw logs.

The log home kit industry actually started about 50 years ago as Bruce Ward, who built his first log home in 1923, began building for others in 1931. Bruce set up a mill for his cedar logs in Presque Isle, Maine. Business wasn't overwhelming, but it did keep him busy until World War II when he stopped log production and began manufacturing materials for the war effort.

Industry growth continued slowly until the 1970s. In 1977 the Log Homes Council, a division of the National Association of Home Manufacturers, was formed; it now represents 21 major log home manufacturers in the United States. Experts say there are as many as 200 manufacturers in the U.S. and Canada, most of whom sell primarily to regional markets.

The industry is growing up with log grading standards and studies on thermal efficiency of logs and wood preservatives. Manufacturers are developing prefabricated log walls and modular log homes as well as new joint designs for improved energy efficiency.

4

This book will describe construction of log homes from both rough logs and kits. Each has advantages and disadvantages. The bravest do-it-yourself log home builder is one who will cut the trees, season them, hand-peel them, treat them, and design and build his own log home completely from scratch with little outside help—a true pioneer.

Few realize that it may be more efficient to hire someone else to do some or all of these tasks. You, as builder, have the option of purchasing standing timber on someone else's property and logging it or having it logged off. You can also purchase it from a local logger or miller trimmed to the desired shape and size. You can even hire a log home builder and work as his assistant in building the home from

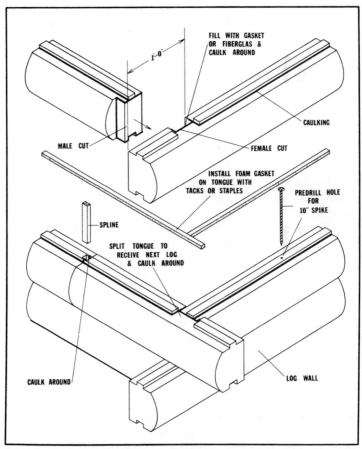

Fig. 1-5. Milled logs are simpler to install than rough logs, but more costly (courtesy Northern Products Log Homes, Inc.).

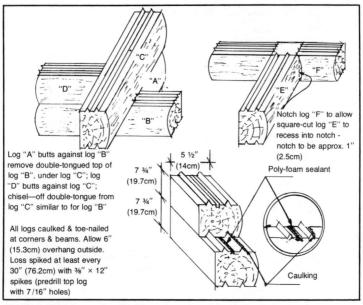

Log "A" butts against log "B" remove double-tongued top of log "B", under log "C"; log "D" butts against log "C"; chisel—off double-tongue from log "C" similar to for log "B"

All logs caulked & toe-nailed at corners & beams. Allow 6" (15.3cm) overhang outside. Loss spiked at least every 30" (76.2cm) with ⅜" × 12" spikes (predrill top log with 7/16" holes)

Notch log "F" to allow square-cut log "E" to recess into notch - notch to be approx. 1" (2.5cm)

Poly-foam sealant

Caulking

5 ½" (14cm)

7 ¾" (19.7cm)

7 ¾" (19.7cm)

Fig. 1-6. Double-notch milled logs (courtesy Lincoln Logs Ltd.).

scratch. Or you can attend a log home building school and learn the techniques of planning and building your own home. We'll consider each.

Building from scratch requires about a year—six months for cutting and seasoning of the logs and six months for construction and finishing. Of course, much depends on the size of the home, available manpower, available time, and the weather. Thorough seasoning of logs and part-time construction can stretch the timetable to three years. Construction with the aid of an experienced crew and preseasoned logs can be completed within three months or less. Construction from rough logs requires fewer tools and less expense than does a conventional frame home.

Log homes also come in kit form that can be constructed by the owner or a contractor. There are actually two kinds of kits: basic (or shell) and full kits. The basic kit includes the logs used in constructing exterior or shell walls and hardware such as spikes and joint gaskets to seal the logs together. Full kits come in degrees of "fullness"—that is, some full kits include everything from tongue-and-groove flooring to ridge shingles. They may have dimensional lumber for interior walls and even ready-to-hang cabinets. Other "full" kits include only windows and doors, some flooring, stair kits, and other basic components.

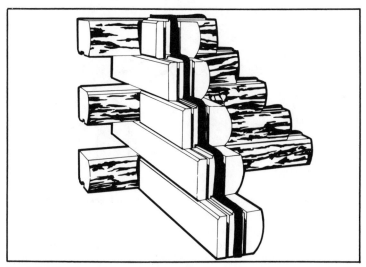

Fig. 1-7. Milled log notches are designed both to seal and to make construction easier (courtesy New England Log Homes, Inc.).

The less-than complete full kit allows you to purchase stock components (such as doors and windows, cabinets, and roofing) closer to your building site. This saves you the cost of transportating these materials, a major consideration when the log home factory is a thousand miles away. With a full coordinated building package you pay the extra transportation costs but do not have to spend time locating, purchasing, and transporting materials.

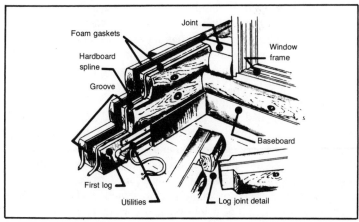

Fig. 1-8. The grooves cut in each log are filled with a hardbound spline and sealed with two weatherproof foam gaskets (courtesy Real Log Homes, Inc.).

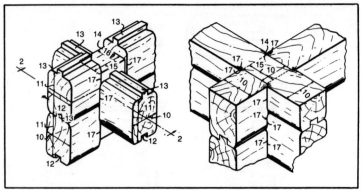

Fig. 1-9. Some log kit manufacturers offer fully milled timbers for ease of construction (courtesy Pan Abode Cedar Homes).

With a kit you get blueprints, material lists, and a construction guide. Some manufacturers also provide technical assistance either on-site or over a WATS line to kit builders and contractors. You pay for these extras, but they can save you time, effort, and money if you run into problems. No special skills are needed to build a shell package, but you may need to hire subcontractors for electrical, plumbing, and other work depending on your own skills and local building codes. Even if you hire a contractor to build you a turn-key log home, you should be familiar with log home construction, so keep reading.

WHY LOGS?

Wood is a natural building component because it is strong, workable, and readily available. It can be used whole or cut up into dimensional lumber. Each form has its own advantages.

There are three types of "logs" used in log homes. *Whole logs* use the structure and basic shape of the original tree as a form for the log. They are trees that are either hand or machine peeled and naturally tapered or machine tapered for a uniform size. Most log homes (both kit and scratch) use whole logs. *Stacked timber* is dimensional lumber that is milled and notched to fit together snugly. It offers many of the construction and aesthetic advantages of the whole log home while giving a more conventional look to walls. The *half log* or *siding log* is used as siding on a conventional frame wall to give it the appearance of whole-log construction. This book will illustrate construction of whole log and stacked timber homes.

Log construction is particularly suited for the do-it-yourselfer because building log walls combines six traditional construction

Fig. 1-10. A double-notch cedar timber (courtesy Justus Homes).

steps into one. The stack-type log wall replaces framing, insulating, exterior sheathing, siding, interior covering, and finishing. The disadvantage to this is that utilities must be routed through logs or, preferably, through interior framed walls.

"Rustic beauty" is a term often used by log home owners, prospects, and manufacturers. Many build log homes simply for the natural appearance and charm of log texture and design. In a time

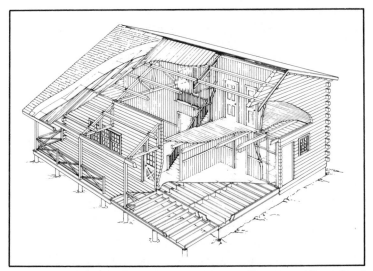

Fig. 1-11. Most log home kits use a combination of milled logs and dimensional lumber (courtesy Northeastern Log Homes).

Fig. 1-12. Log homes can be as large and spacious as any other custom home (courtesy Real Log Homes, Inc.).

when homeowners must nail numbers to their houses to distinguish them from their neighbors', people are searching for new ways to make a statement about themselves and their lifestyle. The log home offers one such option.

Log homes are also popular because they blend well into rural settings—they are appropriate. In fact, 85 percent of all log homes are built on rural sites. Even so, a few manufacturers have developed log home subdivisions and many businesses are housed in log shopping centers.

Another reason for the growing popularity of log homes is their energy efficiency. The combination of the cellular structure of wood and the six to twelve inch thick walls offer a built-in passive solar system that industry experts estimate is about 25 percent more heat efficient than similar frame houses.

The industry is having some trouble proving this fact because most insulation codes are regulated by "R-factors." An *R-factor* is the thermal insulating ability of a material compared to air. When the R-factor of a material is tested, it is done under laboratory conditions: 72 degrees Fahrenheit in 0 percent humidity. The moisture content of wood exposed to atmosphere is about 15 percent (higher in humid regions). It's like testing apples against bananas. HUD and the Department of Energy are now testing log, frame, and masonry homes for thermal efficiency.

Much of the energy efficiency of log walls comes from their ability to retain heat and cold for long periods. They become energy walls that hold the night's coolness for release throughout the day and the daytime warmth for the night.

Fig. 1-13. Many efficient log homes are two or more stories tall (courtesy Ward Cabin Co., Inc.).

In addition to this property, a number of log home manufacturers have introduced passive and active solar designs for log homes to increase efficiency and reduce heating and cooling bills. Designs are also available for those who build their log home from scratch to take advantage of solar technology at reduced costs.

Another reason for increased interest in log homes is low maintenance. Many woods (especially the cedars) are naturally decay-resistant and only require treatment every 10 to 20 years. Even the pines need treatment only every few years with a preservative. Painting isn't required, though some log home owners add to the rustic look with redwood stain. The primary preservative is

Fig. 1-14. Even businesses can be housed in log buildings (courtesy Ward Cabin Co., Inc.).

Fig. 1-15. Log homes can combine rustic beauty and modern charm (courtesy Justus Homes).

applied before the walls are built, either at the site or at the factory. Some log homes are never treated, but allowed to weather naturally and discolor from sun and rain. Yet they still outlive many conventional frame homes.

Log home construction costs can be high. Many log home builders find that final costs are 10 to 25 percent higher than they expected. The problem is not the log home, but the *builder*. As the home takes form, additions and changes are made that are tacked on to the cost of building—a wall is moved; additional insulation is added; a higher grade of carpeting is installed. With each change, the costs mount.

But overall, the cost of a log home is approximately the same as an identical custom frame home, all else being equal. That is, if you have a contractor build your log home it will be about the same price per square foot as a similar frame home with the same amenities.

Where you *can* save is in labor. You may know nothing about framing a home, but nearly anyone can erect log walls and reduce the labor costs. You can use your family and friends to erect walls in a matter of days. The savings can be used to enlarge your home or add amenities you may not otherwise be able to afford.

Of course, construction costs can be further reduced by building your log home from scratch, cutting and curing logs now on your property or available inexpensively standing on another property.

12

The more you do yourself, the less you'll have to buy from others. Framing a conventional home is more complicated and offers less opportunity for securing low-cost materials and do-it-yourself labor.

Another advantage of log homes—and all custom homes—is that you can build them as simple or as ornate as you (and your pocketbook) desire. The so-called "spec home" built by most contractors is a home that guesses at what the average person will buy. It's a compromise. Your log home may be more Spartan, include a larger master bedroom and smaller children's rooms, a sewing room/den, a single garage, or other features that reflect *your* current and projected lifestyle rather than that of the "average" family. You can dictate the costs and features more closely when you build your own home.

There's a side benefit of direct cost reduction: mortgage reduction. That is, as you lower costs of building your home through efficient designing or low-cost labor, you can also reduce the cost of your mortgage in two ways.

The first mortgage reduction is in the total amount you borrow. Your labor input can reduce the mortgage by 20 percent or more. That means your "$50,000 mortgage" need only be for $40,000. That's a savings of more than just $10,000. Over the 30 year life of a 14 percent mortgage, that's a savings of *more than $42,000* in

Fig. 1-16. Open beam ceilings give a spacious look (courtesy Beaver Log Homes).

Fig. 1-17. The log home kitchen can look as rustic or modern as the owner desires (courtesy Beaver Log Homes).

principal and interest. A great deal depends on your down payment and your labor input or "sweat equity," but any home that can allow you to reduce labor costs will pay dividends in mortgage relief.

The second mortgage reduction comes from earning a lower interest rate with a greater equity in your home. If you're building an $80,000 home and you only need a mortgage of $40,000—a 50 percent mortgage—to build because of your sweat and land equities, you can earn a reduced mortgage rate. That is, you may be able to find a bank who will rent you the money at 13 percent rather than 14 percent because of the reduced risk of your high equity ownership. One percent of interest doesn't sound like much until you figure it out. On a $40,000 mortgage, it's $31.47 in interest each month—more than $11,300 saved in 30 years!

The problem is that log homes are new to many banks and financing can be difficult to find. Your high equity position will help you find the lowest cost financing in your area. (We'll talk more about costs and financing of your log home in Chapter 4.)

There's one other important reason why people buy and build log homes: pride of ownership. Many homeowners feel that the more efficient use of God's resources is a source of pride. They know that about half of the wood used in milling dimensional lumber winds up as wood chips, a usable but less efficient by-product.

Fig. 1-18. Interior walls can be covered with tongue-and-groove pine to retain the solid wood look of a log home.

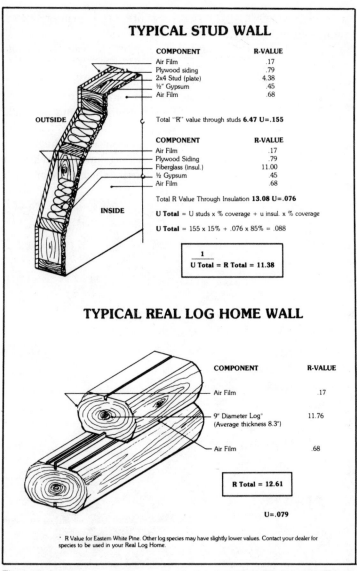

TYPICAL STUD WALL

COMPONENT	R-VALUE
Air Film	.17
Plywood siding	.79
2x4 Stud (plate)	4.38
½" Gypsum	.45
Air Film	.68

Total "R" value through studs **6.47 U=.155**

COMPONENT	R-VALUE
Air Film	.17
Plywood Siding	.79
Fiberglass (insul.)	11.00
½ Gypsum	.45
Air Film	.68

Total R Value Through Insulation **13.08 U=.076**

U Total = U studs x % coverage + u insul. x % coverage

U Total = 155 x 15% + .076 x 85% = .088

$$\frac{1}{\text{U Total}} = \text{R Total} = 11.38$$

OUTSIDE

INSIDE

TYPICAL REAL LOG HOME WALL

COMPONENT	R-VALUE
Air Film	.17
9" Diameter Log* (Average thickness 8.3")	11.76
Air Film	.68

R Total = 12.61

U=.079

* R Value for Eastern White Pine. Other log species may have slightly lower values. Contact your dealer for species to be used in your Real Log Home.

Fig. 1-19. Comparison of R-factors of typical stud and log walls (courtesy Beaver Log Homes).

There's very little waste in the milling of logs for homes. There's also a pride in being a part of the building of a home, whether it be strictly as a designer and sidewalk supervisor, or as a wall builder, or as the complete builder from foundation to chimney cap.

Fig. 1-20. Lofts can be added to increase living space and reduce costs (courtesy New England Log Homes, Inc.).

There's also an ego trip to saying "Yes, I live in a log home." It's a sense of individuality that's difficult to find in a spec home or even in most custom homes.

And finally, there's the resale value. Log homes that are professionally built (by you or a contractor) retain their value and often improve with age. The log home built ten or more years ago is

Fig. 1-21. Most log home kit manufacturers are located where the trees are (courtesy Northeastern Log Homes).

Fig. 1-22. Log home kits ready for delivery (courtesy Northeastern Log Homes).

usually more beautiful than the one built last month. The resale market is usually good due to the demand for log homes and the desire of many to save the headaches of building one and working out the bugs.

Those are the reasons why people buy and build log homes: natural beauty, energy efficiency, low maintenance, construction costs, mortgage relief, pride of ownership. There are disadvantages, too, and we'll look at them as we consider the steps to log home ownership.

ROUGH LOGS OR KIT?

By way of introduction, let's look at the steps to building your log home from both rough logs and a kit. This will be an overview; the actual step-by-step construction of your log home is thoroughly outlined in Chapters 2 through 15.

If you plan to do much of the building yourself, you'll first need a good source of wood and other materials. The logs can be cut from your building site, or purchased from nearby landowners or public property on contract and logged off by you or a professional logger. The local wood may be the right species for your log construction or it may not. (There will be more on selecting and cutting your timber in Chapter 2.)

The next step is to develop your plans for your log home and site. You can either do them yourself or hire the plans drawn by a local architect, log architect specialist, or log home manufacturer. Try for a specialist or manufacturer's engineering department who understands the special needs and problems of log homes: bending, compression and tensile strengths, checking, compaction, and moisture. Choose your site and plan it out before you begin clearing it to save as much of the natural landscaping as possible.

The next step is the planning of construction. Building from rough logs can be more difficult than kit logs because they are often larger, need to be cured, peeled, milled, and sealed. Careful planning is the answer. Decide how and where you will treat and prepare your logs, how you will hoist them to the wall, how you will fasten them in place, where you will cut windows and allow for doors. Think ahead.

Finally, consider your tools and labor. How many workers can you expect to have during construction? One person can build a log home with planning and technology, but it's much easier with a crew of two to five. Check the tool lists in Chapters 2 and 6 to find out what you have and what you need.

Building from scratch can offer you savings over building from a kit. By doing much of the labor yourself you can reduce costs. Finding, cutting, curing, and preparing your own logs can also give you a knowledge of your home that few frame or even log kit homeowners have. However, building from rough logs can often be more headache than one person—or an entire family—wants to take on. The selection and preparation of good building logs is hard work,

Fig. 1-23. Wood is milled and stacked inside a log home factory (courtesy Justus Homes).

Fig. 1-24. Milling logs into timbers (courtesy Northeastern Log Homes).

and many would prefer to trade their labor at their normal occupation for the labor of a professional log home builder or kit manufacturer—making the transfer of labor with money. Some of the headaches that arise in building from scratch include lining up and training workers, securing materials on time, engineering problems of building walls and roofs, treating logs, and managing the project.

Buying a kit log home can solve some, but not all, of the problems of building from scratch. Log selection and preparation is taken care of by the manufacturer who will choose the species and specific trees based on two criteria: wood characteristics and proximity to his mill. That problem is solved for you.

In shopping for a kit, though, be aware of what is included and what isn't. Are you purchasing a shell package or a complete kit? How complete? Does it include materials for interior frame walls? What plumbing is included? As mentioned earlier, the complete kit can be a good buy as long as it doesn't have to be transported far from the factory with trucking costs eating up the benefits.

Once the kit is chosen and the materials for local purchase are identified, you need to gather the financing and plan for delivery. Terms for the kit are cash on delivery, with a quarter to a third of the package price payable when ordering and the rest when the kit package arrives at your site. Of course, much of this may be handled by your contractor and your banker so all you have to do is supervise construction.

The advantage of building your log home from a kit is that the manufacturer has done much of the selection and preparation of the wood. He has also developed a general construction guide and may even offer a factory representative or dealer to assist you. This support is more expensive than doing it entirely by yourself, but it can be more efficient if you're not familiar with log construction.

The convenience of the kit is another advantage. When your kit arrives it will probably have numbered logs and complete assembly instructions. Windows are precut. Corners are notched and logs are jointed, milled, and peeled. Much of the more difficult and time-consuming work is already done. It's then a simple matter to stack the logs into walls as instructed and begin building your log home.

One of the problems is that most log home manufacturers don't season or cure their wood. The majority of logs are milled while they are still "green" or unseasoned. They haven't fully dried out. This can cause problems once the logs are in place as they dry. Some will bow or twist unless they are heavily spiked into place. The solution is to get wood that's as dry as possible and secure it well when it's installed.

Another disadvantage of kits (and with *all* log homes) is securing financing. Most bankers don't even want to talk with do-it-yourself home builders and may not even be willing to work with contractors who are not thoroughly familiar with the special problems of log home construction. Since you'll need to finance more money if you buy a kit than if you build from scratch, the bankers are more difficult to work with. There are ways around this problem and they will be outlined in Chapter 4 on estimating construction costs.

Fig. 1-25. Trusses are pre-assembled at the factory (courtesy Northeastern Log Homes).

Fig. 1-26. Assembling a timber truss (courtesy Northeastern Log Homes).

QUESTIONS AND ANSWERS

That's an overview of log home construction. Here are answers to the most common questions asked by those who are considering building a log home.

If the walls are solid, how do I get utilities into the rooms? There are many ways of wiring and plumbing your home, depending on the type of logs you use, the composition of your floor and interior walls, and the design of your home. Some kit logs are hollow inside using air as an insulator and so that wires and pipes can be run through them. The builder simply plans ahead and drills vertical holes in the logs as they are stacked. The problem is a little more difficult with whole log construction. The solution is to keep the utilities in outside walls to a minimum, running them under floors and behind interior framed walls. Some plugs can be cut into the "base" log that runs along the floor starting the wall. Other wiring can be run through channels cut in the ends of logs that are in doorways and windows which will later be covered by casings. Utilities to the second story are often run through specially built walls and closets.

What wood species should I choose? Nearly every type of tree has been used to build a log home at one time or another. However, the conifers (evergreens) have the best combination of strength, weight, and workability. The most popular conifers are pine, fir, cedar, and spruce. Each has its own advantages and devotees. Cedar is the most decay-resistant, but is also more difficult to cut and mill. Pine, fir, and spruce are easier to work with but should be treated with a wood preservative for long life. Different species of woods have their own unique characteristics, too. White pine has a higher resistence to decay than red pine, for example. The best wood for your log home is often one that is used by the majority of log home builders in your area—check around. (More on selecting woods in Chapter 2.)

Does it cost more to order a custom-designed kit rather than a stock plan? Generally, no. Most manufacturers admit that less than half of their orders are for stock plan log homes. The majority are modifications or entirely new designs. If the changes are minimal, most kit dealers won't charge for the changes. However, new designs that require computer time and additional engineering may cost slightly more. Get a quote on design charges before you get very serious with any manufacturer.

Can I really build a log home myself? Maybe. Ask yourself a few honest questions: What's the last thing you built? What were the results? Did you complete the project? Do you have any construction knowledge? How much? Have you ever worked with wood before—cutting firewood, felling trees, making furniture, building homes? How much time do you have? Would you feel better working under the guidance of a log contractor? Where can you get experienced labor? How much support does the manufacturer or dealer offer? Are there experienced log home builders in your area who will give technical assistance? If it's just knowledge that's stopping you from building your log home from scratch, you can take a few courses in log home construction offered in many regions. Or you may elect to have a contractor do some or all of the work. Be realistic.

Log homes aren't for everyone. They have their own special problems and situations in both construction and ownership. But a thorough study of this book will give you a complete look at log home construction and help you decide whether log home ownership is for you—and how to go about it.

Chapter 2

Preparing Logs

Whether you build your home from your own trees or purchase a kit, you should understand how logs are chosen, kit, felled, topped and limbed, cribbed and cured, peeled, shaped, and preserved.

Man has yet to invent a building material as versatile and workable as wood. If you look at a piece of wood under a microscope you will see that it's made up of thousands of hollow cells. These natural building blocks are formed from tiny cellulose fibers—about *three million* per cubic inch. They are cemented together by a natural glue called *lignin*.

One of the most surprising qualities of wood is its incredible strength. Pound for pound it's stronger than steel. And thanks to the elastic lignin glue, it can withstand high stress better than most building materials.

Best of all, wood is a readily-available and renewable resource. A large tree can grow from seed to cutting within a man's lifetime.

Wood is also a natural insulator—six times better than brick, 15 times better than concrete, and an astonishing 1770 times better than aluminum. That's why a wood-frame house will keep you warmer in winter and cooler in summer than a masonry home. Experts claim that a log wall will insulate even better than wood-frame wall with fiberglass insulation.

Many woods are also highly decay-resistent, especially if they are thoroughly dried before installation as log walls. In fact, a number of log homes still stand in New England more than 300 winters after they were built. Even the less decay-resistant woods can be treated with synthetic resins and preservatives to increase their life many times.

TREES FOR LOG BUILDING

If you're into numbers, there are somewhere between 60,000 and 70,000 species of trees in the world, with about 850 species native to the United States. We can break them into two classifications: *evergreens* and *deciduous*. Evergreens are year-round trees that drop their leaves as they die and replace them with new ones. The deciduous trees drop their leaves—primarily in the fall and usually in your yard. Most log homes are built with evergreen trees so we'll concentrate on these and narrow them down to the most popular models.

The *broad-leaf* evergreen trees, like the palm, are found in tropical and some temperate areas. They are usually not considered for logs or manufacturing, but rather are used for decoration.

The *needle-leaf* evergreen is native to cooler climates and is used for most building and wood processing. The needle leaf evergreens, called *conifers*, include pine, fir, spruce, cedar, and many other families of trees. They are the most popular with log home builders and manufacturers.

American *cedars* are actually cypress trees. They are highly decay-resistant and easy to work with. The most popular species are Northern White Cedar, Eastern Red Cedar, and Western Red Cedar.

Fig. 2-1. Log homes are an efficient use of our resources (courtesy Wilderness Log Homes).

There are ten species of native *fir* trees in North America, found primarily west of the Rocky Mountains. However, the species that's used most in building log homes, the Douglas fir, is not actually a fir . . . or a pine . . . or a spruce. The Douglas fir is its own species. It's used by many rough log home builders in the western states because of its availability, but few kit manufacturers make it their choice if other species are available.

The *pine* is actually a family of trees that includes the fir, hemlock, larch, spruce, and true cedars. However, most people divide pines into four species: white pine, yellow pine, western yellow or Ponderosa pine, and red pine. White pine is excellent for log home building; it has a high insulation factor, light weight, and excellent workability. The yellow pine is a harder wood and is more difficult to work with, but is still a good log. The western yellow pine is lighter and easier to work with. The red pine is another good wood, but has less resistance to decay.

The *spruce* is an eastern tree. That is, it's found primarily on the east coast of the United States ranging from Canada to Virginia. It comes in three colors—red, white, and black—though the woods actually look very similar. To confuse matters more, the black spruce is also called the yellow spruce. What all spruces have in common is their popularity and their workability. Spruces are much like other conifers in that they are fairly decay-resistant, easy to work with, and readily available. For these reasons, they are popular.

One other species should be mentioned—the *hemlock*. While it isn't used by many kit manufacturers, the western hemlock that grows along the Pacific coast from Alaska to central California is becoming more popular with the log home builder who cuts his own. If treated properly, the western hemlock can make an excellent log home that's fairly light while retaining good insulation qualities.

Of course, the *best* species for your log home is often dictated by what's available. It may be less costly to work around the weaker characteristics of a wood (decay resistance, insulation factor, shrinkage) than to "import" your logs from a distant location where a better species is grown.

WHERE TO GET LOGS

There are many sources of logs other than the kit manufacturers, and since the job of building a log home is labor intensive, the closer you get to the tree itself, the less things will cost. If you can

Fig. 2-2. Thousands of log homes are being built each year (courtesy Ward Cabin Co., Inc.).

log your walls out of the back 40, you can reduce your building costs tremendously.

Unfortunately, not all prospective log home builders have property with the right species, height, and girth for log home construction. In fact, many don't even have enough good wood on the homestead for a winter's supply of firewood. Some must rely on timber from other property, either nearby property they have purchased or property owned by others who are willing to sell timber on the stump.

One way of getting logs is to advertise your need to area property owners with a sign ("Wanted to buy: 12″ Ponderosa Pine on the stump. Will pay cash") on your property or through an ad in the local newspaper. You can also contact Log Brokers and Logging Companies listed in the phone book nearest your building site.

You may also be able to purchase standing timber through the local forest service office. Many have sales of government timber stands that are too small or too remote to interest commercial loggers.

Another excellent source of wall logs is the mill. You may find small lumbermills in your area that will sell you cut logs right out of their workpile. You can find them listed under "Lumber—Mfgs" in the Yellow Pages and in area newspapers. To get the best deal you must know what you're looking for and what you're looking at. That is, if you plan to build with 10 to 16 inch western yellow pine, make sure you know what it looks like and how to grade it. If you don't, hire someone who does for a couple of hours.

If you can do it, timing will get you the best price from the mill. It's best to buy when the mills are the least busy: fall and winter.

Depending on local demand and weather, most mills bring most of their logs in during the spring and do their peak sawing in the spring and summer. Talk with a few local mill operators to find out their peak season and what price reduction you can earn by coming back in the off-season. Some may even do some of the milling for you.

Of course, you'll probably have to arrange for pickup of the logs. Once you've marked your selected logs you can contact logging truck owners in the area (most of whom are independent contractors) to get the best price on hauling.

CRUISING

Time to "cruise." *Cruising* is simply choosing the logs you want for your home while they are still standing or on the pile. You're looking for wood that has the fewest limbs—limbs mean knots. You are also looking for logs of the same circumference and of minimum taper.

Here's how to figure circumference or girth. Say you're looking for 12 inch logs for your finished home. Add two inches of thickness for bark that will be removed. That's 14 inches. Now multiply it by *pi* (3.14) and you will get about 44 inches. Using a tailor's tape you can measure trees for an approximate girth of 44 inches. Ten inch logs plus bark will be 38 inches in girth; 14 inch logs plus bark are about 50 inches around.

Trees will be widest at the base and taper upwards. The idea is to get the *least* taper because a log that's 36 inches around on one end and 52 on the other will require a lot of extra work fitting it into your wall. You may have to climb your chosen tree to get a girth measurement higher up. Of course, if you're going to mill the log flat on two sides, taper won't be as critical.

How can you estimate how tall a tree is? Use a little applied math: Make a visual triangle by extending your arm in a fist, measuring the distance between your sighting eye and the top of your fist, and hold a stick vertically in your hand that same distance above your fist. That is, if your eye and fist are 26 inches apart, make sure the stick stands 26 inches above the top of your hand. You're making an equilateral right triangle with the sighting line as the hypoteneuse. Got that? Now back up until you can see the base of the tree over the top of your hand *and* the top of the tree right at the top of the stick. Now measure the distance between where you are standing and the base of the tree. That's the height of your tree.

Once you've chosen the perfect tree you can mark it for cutting with the perfect marker: a can of spray paint. Red is a good color.

FELLING A TREE

To get your tree from vertical to horizontal you'll need a few tools. Primary tools include saws and wedges. Saws can either be hand saws (such as the one-man timber saw or the two-man crosscut saw) or a power saw. The hand saw has just about been eliminated by the (usually) easier-to-use power saws. In recent years they have become so safe and powerful that today nearly anyone can learn to safely fell a tree within minutes. Axes can also be used to drop trees, but most woodsmen set them aside in favor of the gasoline-driven beaver.

You'll be using other tools as you move, limb, and bark your tree into a log: log dog, drawknife, peeling spud, adze, broadaxe, froe and mallet, scribe, and others. You'll be introduced to them as you need them.

Different seasons are preferred for felling trees. The best for the log home builder is late fall/early winter for three reasons: the sap is lowest and trees are easier to cut; snow will cushion the fall and reduce tree damage; and the fallen tree will have a four to eight month seasoning period before the home is built—usually in the summer months. Of course, your own time schedule may dictate when you cut your trees. It may be in the summer for an early spring building, or it may be year-round because of limited time available for the job.

If possible, fell only absolutely vertical trees on flat ground—at least until you get some experience. Decide which way you want the tree to fall based on clearings, obstacles, snagging limbs, and the wind. You want to get the tree to the ground without breaking or hanging up. If this puts it in a position that will make it easier to get out of the woods, so much the better.

Fig. 2-3. A log home in the woods (courtesy New England Log Homes, Inc.).

Clear the area around the base of the tree so that you have room to maneuver while you're cutting. You'll also want to figure an escape route away from the tree's path and clear of it.

Ready to cut? You'll actually be making two notches in the tree—one in the direction of the fall (called the *notch cut*) and one on the opposite side of the tree (called the *felling cut* or *back cut*). The notch cut is actually two cuts—the *first cut* and the *top cut*. The first cut is made level about a third of the way into the tree. You make the top cut from above the first cut and down at an angle to the back of that first cut. Then you knock the wedge out of the tree and your notch cut is done. If your saw binds during the cut, you can free it with wooden, metal, or plastic wedges driven into the *kerf* or slot.

The felling cut is made on the opposite side of the tree away from the direction it will fall. Make a horizontal cut about two inches higher than the first cut in your notch on the other side. Don't cut all the way through; leave what's called a *hinge*—a two inch thickness of trunk between the notch and felling cuts—to direct the fall and minimize bucking. Without a hinge, a wind could come up against the top of the tree and push it in the wrong direction. *Bucking* is when the cut tree kicks backwards as it falls, possibly hitting someone or changing the fall.

When cutting larger trees you may have to make two cuts out of the felling cut, the first from the side into the heart of the tree and the second keeping the saw's tip in the heart and rotating the blade around the back side of the tree. You may also want to use wedges as you go to keep the blade from binding on the felling cut.

Once the cuts are made, simply drive a wedge into the kerf of the felling cut (see how you quickly pick up the woodsman's lingo?) until the tree begins to fall. Then lay your tools down, quickly check the direction of the fall and move away from its path at an angle of 90 degrees or so to make sure you're not running under it. Think *safety first*.

As you cruise the forest, you'll learn one rule of nature: The perfect tree always grows in a poor location. Once you've had some experience at felling the easier trees you can tackle a few of the more difficult ones.

Your chosen tree may grow leaning heavily in one direction. Once you've decided that it can be safely dropped in that direction, bind the tree with a chain a foot above your intended cut, because the tree will want to fall before you complete your felling cut. To relieve this pressure, it will probably split and crack, damaging usable wood. The chain girdle will minimize the loss. Next, make a side cut on each side of the trunk to minimize tearing. Then make

Fig. 2-4. Porches add both a rustic look and a direction for future expansion (courtesy New England Log Homes, Inc.).

the notch cut on the side on which you want the tree to fall. Finally, make the felling cut on the back side. Be ready to use your planned escape route, because a heavily leaning tree starts the fall quicker than a vertical one.

Once you're a proven woodsman, you can try felling a tree in a direction other than the way it's leaning. This starts with a notch cut on the side of the tree that will fall first. Then make your felling cut with one important difference: The hinge should be a triangle rather than a rectangle. The narrow end of the hinge will point in the direction of the lean. Finally, place the wedges into the kerf from the side that's leaning and drive them in to both start the fall and keep it from falling toward the lean.

All woodsmen have a healthy respect for a tree that's hung up in another tree during the fall. These are unpredictable. They can be minimized by carefully checking each tree you choose; determine whether its higher limbs are tied into another tree and whether the falling path is blocked by snagging limbs that would stop the tree. If your tree gets hung up, get help. You'll need to tie it into other trees and top it or, preferably, carefully cut the offending tree down.

One more rule for the woods: A windy day is your day off. Don't try to esimate what a wind 50 feet above you will do to your tree once it's cut. It may defy all the rules and drop it right where you least expect it.

FROM TREE TO LOG

Once your tree is on the ground you can begin working it into a log that will eventually become part of your home. You'll cut the top off, trim the limbs away, haul it to your storage site, stack it with others for drying, and peel and shape it.

To *limb* your tree you'll need only your chain saw. Standing on one side of the fallen tree, cut the limbs off the opposite side (for safety). Small limbs can be trimmed with a single cut. Larger limbs should be cut with a *top cut* and an *under cut*. The first cut should be the one on the side that the limb will go once it's cut—that is, the under cut is normally made first about a third of the way into the limb, then the top cut finishes it off. However, if the limb is under pressure and will break away *against* gravity, make the top cut first, and then the releasing under cut.

Bucking is simply sawing the felled tree into logs. You may have decided on a specific length that is easiest to transport, cure, and use (such as 16 feet). Or you may have the equipment to haul and store logs up to 35 feet in length. Do whatever's convenient.

There are two kinds of bucking: *overbucking* and *underbucking*. Overbucking is cutting down from the top of the log, while under-bucking is cutting up from the underside. To decide which way to cut or buck your tree, check the stress and consider which way the tree would move if it were cut completely through. Would both halves drop? If so, make the top cut first and finish with an under cut. Would one half drop and the other kick up? Then start with an under cut and finish with a top cut. Plan ahead, be alert, and *think safety*.

HAULING

It's time to haul your logs out of the woods. Full logs can weigh from 300 to 1000 pounds or more, especially right after they are cut, when the moisture content is high. There are many ways of hauling logs, the *best* one depending on available equipment and the remoteness of your logging site. A few *twitching* teams still pull logs out of the woods with horses, but most logs are dragged or *skidded* out with mechanical horses: logging trucks with self-loaders, Jeeps and other four-wheel drive vehicles, tractors and block and tackle.

A stout chain can be attached to your vehicle and then to the log with either grapple hooks that dig into the log or a skidding pan placed under one end of the log. Another method is to lift one end of the log with a tractor bucket.

Before skidding your logs out of the woods, plan your path and clear it of obstacles like fallen trees, heavy brush, and rocks. Choose a path that is level or as near to level as possible to minimize work. Avoid crossing river beds or ravines. It's easier to go around an obstacle than cross it.

Some smart log home builders kill two birds with one stone by cutting a road to their future building site, felling trees in the way.

Then, after the stumps are removed, the logs can be pulled along the road to the site. Of course, not all properties are set up for this time-saving method.

As you've learned, newly-cut trees have high moisture and sap content. Once they are cut they begin to dry out. That's good *and* bad. The good is that dry rot (a misnomer; it should be called *wet* rot) breeds in wood with a moisture content over 30 percent, and that's most newly cut trees. They begin to dry out and lose their susceptibility to dry rot once they are down. The bad part is that many woods also shrink and change shape once they dry out. Then you have bowed logs, which are very difficult to work with.

The answer to this problem is to stack the logs in such a way that they have air circulating around them without undergoing stress that will magnify or encourage bowing. This is called *cribbing*. Cribbing is started by stacking the first course of logs a few inches off the ground, using scrap logs of equal thickness as the base. Allowing circulation space between each log, you can put many in the same layer, then cross-layer logs of similar thickness. If you stack them one above another, you will minimize the stress on the separating log.

Another answer is to not cure them at all. Some builders feel that the best place for them to dry into shape is on the wall itself. Once the logs come to the building site they peel and notch them, then begin building the walls. These builders spike them in place and let them dry right on the wall. This works as long as adequate space is allowed for shrinkage and compaction of the wall when building window and door frames and interior walls.

Fig. 2-5. Increasing the roof height and pitch adds an efficient loft area for living or storage (courtesy Ward Cabin Co., Inc.).

Some builders peel logs before they crib them and some wait until after. Peeling discourages parasites that live in the bark from taking over much of the log. Peeling also hastens drying, but fast drying increases *checking*—the cracking lines in wood. It's a matter of time and taste.

Most log home builders feel that the best time to peel your logs is in the spring, especially after the bark has had a few months to dry out. They start out with a bark peeling spud that's forced between the bark and the wood; this is much like peeling a potato with a flat-edged spoon. The spuds can be purchased from logging suppliers or made from an old shovel with a flattened nose.

The next step is to finish the bark off with a drawknife. The drawknife strips away the final layer of bark skin and gives the log a hand-hewn look that is difficult to match with milling methods. The drawknife is pulled toward you to shave and smooth the log surface.

There are two tools that you'll need to move and hold your logs as you peel and draw them. They are the *cant hook* and *log dogs*. Such colorful names echo back to earlier days when these were necessary tools in the homesteader's shed. The cant hook is a pole with a spiked hook at one end. It's used to move logs short distances. Log dogs are three-foot iron bars with turned points at each end that can be driven into logs to hold them into place. They are not necessary tools, but they are useful.

The next step is shaping the logs so that they will stack easily into walls. Flattened logs are much easier to work with than round ones and they seal better. Flattened logs are also more uniform in height, making the stacking simpler. There are three ways to flatten your logs:

Hand-hew two sides of the logs. The logs are first scored with a hand axe, then hewn flat with a broadaxe, and finally smoothed with an adze. This is a laborous process, but preferred by "traditional" log home builders.

Chain saw. Using a timber spiked onto the log as a guide, you can draw the chain saw along the log, ripping off one face. Then you turn it over and rip the opposite face. Your log is now flattened.

Mill. You can also have a mill rip your logs—either a stationary mill or a portable mill that comes to your building site. Builders who purchase their logs from a mill can sometimes get the mill to flatten the logs at a small additional cost.

If you prefer not to flatten your logs, you can *cup* them by cutting a channel along one side so that it will sit atop the log below it on the wall. This is best done as the wall is being constructed to ensure a custom fit.

Fig. 2-6. Log homes make a comfortable place to sit out the winter (courtesy Ward Cabin Co., Inc.).

Once the log is flattened, most builders groove the level sides to insert a wood spline to fit and seal with the next log.

PRESERVING LOGS

Most woods need synthetic preservatives to keep them from being destroyed by insects and rot. Cedar logs—actually American cypress—are the most resistant to decay and can last 20 years or more without preservatives. However, most woods should be treated with a preservative prior to construction.

The most common preservative is *penta*. It's an oil-based preservative that's safe for both interior and exterior use. *Creosote* is also used, but is only safe for exterior applications. Other common preservatives include *copper napthenate* and *chromated zinc chloride*.

The best way to apply your preservative is by soaking the logs in it for about five minutes. This is difficult when you're working with large logs. You can build a trough out of scrap lumber, line it with aluminum, and caulk it. Or you can build one from halved oil drums welded together. Make sure you turn the log in the preservative so that it soaks into the wood fiber.

You can also spray or brush on the preservative, but this isn't very effective and must be repeated every few years. Some builders just varnish the wood and pray for the best. We'll talk more about maintaining your logs with preservatives in Chapter 16.

GOING BACK TO SCHOOL

There's one attractive alternative when building from scratch: the log home building school. There are many such schools throughout the United States and Canada that offer resident student courses in material selection and acquisition, selection, use and maintenance of tools, log lifting techniques and devices, construction safety, and interior finishing. There are courses for both beginners and intermediate log home builders.

One such school is B. Allan Mackie's School of Log Building in Prince George, British Columbia, Canada. The General Session is two weeks long and follows the basic outline of instruction developed in Mackie's excellent book, *Building With Logs*. The school also offers a regular course for graduates to brush up on the newest log building techniques, as well as one day seminars. Their address is P.O. Box 1205, Prince George, B.C., Canada V2L4V3.

Another school is the Legendary Log Home School at Sisters, Oregon, in the Northwest's Cascade Mountains. Typical three-week courses offer detailed instruction in site selection and preparation, foundation preparation and construction, flooring, wall construction, and roofing. Another course is offered in finishing techniques. Write them at P.O. Box 1150, Sisters, OR 97759.

Other log home construction schools can be found in the Log Home Guide, published quarterly by Muir Publishing Co., Ltd., Gardenvale, Que, Canada H9X1BO. Their U.S. address is 56 Clarendon Ave., W. Rutland, VT 05777. It's an excellent publication for the do-it-yourself log home builder.

It's a hearty soul who decides to build his—or her—own log home from scratch. It *can* be done and it *is being* done. All it takes is knowledge and perseverence.

Chapter 3

Designing Your Log Home

One of the most enjoyable aspects of planning and building your own log home is designing it to meet your individual needs and tastes. You can give your log home its own personality and make it unique.

The task of designing your log home isn't as difficult as you might think. It's simply applying basic architectural laws and techniques to solve your particular problems of how to stay warm, comfortable, and happy. It *does* require a lot of thought and evaluation.

The primary purpose of your home is to provide you and your family with cost-effective shelter. Nearly any home can fulfill this objective, but individuality in homes comes from fulfilling secondary purposes: status, recreation, seclusion, uniqueness, work space, comfort. So the best place to start your design is by reviewing your family's current and projected lifestyle.

DESIGNING FOR LIFESTYLE

The first question to ask is: What activities are in your family's lifestyle? That is, are you outdoor-oriented, preferring open spaces and less interior room, or are you homebodies who like to read and work quietly in natural-tone rooms? Are you planning a pool, stable, large workshop, canning room, or nearby airstrip?

Do you expect this activity pattern to change in the next few years? Do you expect to retire in this home? If so, what activities will fill your days? Are they indoor or outdoor?

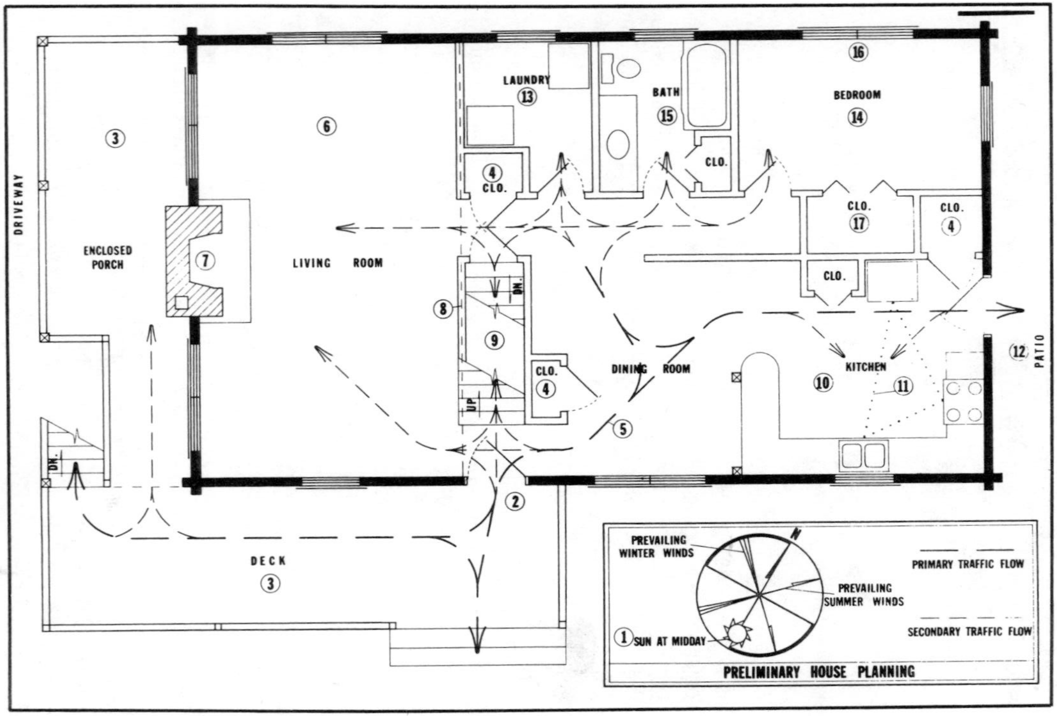

Fig. 3-1. Design your log home for efficient traffic flow and siting (courtesy Northern Products Log Homes, Inc.).

Also consider secondary activities. You may be the outdoors type but also need a small shop where you can make gun stocks and reload ammunition. Or you may have a home business, but also enjoy throwing patio parties. Take a close look at your family today and in the coming years to decide what you would like in your log home.

Look at the home you're in *now* and consider what you like and what you'd change about it. Get the family together to gather ideas. Review not only likes and dislikes of your current home, but also of homes you frequent—friends, relatives, neighbors. Consider traffic, furniture, rooms, room size and placement, home styles, heating, and cooling.

Traffic is simply how people move from one place to another. You'll notice that in your present home there are some locations that get more use than others. Others are passed through but not used. Principal traffic flow will generally occur through the heart of the living area. It's sometimes best to reroute this traffic out of the living room itself.

There should be a clear division between the living area (living room, kitchen, family room) and the bedrooms so that the bedrooms are quiet and private. Buffer zones such as halls, closets, and storage help break the busy and private portions of the home. This separation can also be achieved in a two-story design with bedrooms upstairs and living area downstairs.

When considering traffic, bathrooms should always be on the path to the bedroom; don't make it bedroom, *then* bath. Visitors can then use facilities without having to pass or cross through a bedroom area. If there are two baths on the same floor (such as one in the hallway and one off the master bedroom), keep them back-to-back if possible to reduce plumbing costs. For additional efficiency, place utility rooms near bathrooms to minimize piping.

Will there be heavy traffic from the front door to back door because of a pool or patio? If so, route traffic around the house to reduce interior wear. Also, if you're building a two-story home, remember to place the laundry room near the stairs—or install a clothes chute. Your stairway should be located near the center of the house and easily accessible from all points.

Consider your furniture. Will you be moving your present furniture into your new log home? What will you be adding? Dropping? What styles do you prefer? Colors? These factors are all important in your final design. You may decide to work a sectional sofa into a conversation pit in the new living room. Or you may decide to frame over one or more exterior log walls so you can use wallpaper that will better match your furniture. You may have antiques that you want to work into your log home design in an entryway or expanded master bedroom. Or do you plan to chuck it all and build your own wood furniture?

Again, you have to look into the future to decide what your lifestyle and furniture needs will be in the next few years. Will you be replacing that electric stove with an antique wood stove in a few years? Then you'd better plan a nearby wood room. When Junior leaves home do you plan to take out his waterbed and speaker brackets and set up a dress design studio? You may want to plan outside stairs for both Junior and yourself.

CHOOSING YOUR ROOMS

Let's put some of these ideas into practice by deciding exactly what rooms you'll need in your log home. This is important because an unused room is wasted money—money that could have been spent on a larger fireplace or wood stove, more energy-efficient windows, or a larger deck. And a cramped home is just as wasteful.

Let's start with bedrooms. The size of many homes is dictated by the number of bedrooms. If you'll only be living in your log home during the summer months, you may be able to get away with one bedroom for the adults and one for the kids. However, most families perfer at least one for adults, one for boys, and another for girls. Those with more money can provide one bedroom for each child.

Some families prefer to have guests over periodically and

Fig. 3-2. The number and size of bedrooms is a primary design factor (courtesy New England Log Homes, Inc.).

Fig. 3-3. The living room should be designed after considering present and future needs (courtesy New England Log Homes, Inc.).

include a guest bedroom in their plans. Others set up a folding bed or sleeper sofa in the living room, family room, or den. Families who expect to expand should include an extra bedroom in their plans and use it for storage or a den until it's needed.

The weighing factor in this is cost. Each bedroom will cost $4000, to $5000 to build, excluding supportive rooms like additional baths and larger family and dining rooms. It's easy to plan for six bedrooms in your dream home; it's much harder to pay for them.

Bathrooms are next. If your log home has two or even three bedrooms on the same floor you may get away with just one bath, depending on your needs and your pocketbook. However, if you go to two floors you'll certainly need at least two baths, one up and one down. Large baths or small? Tubs, showers, or both? Single or double sink? Dressing area? Think it over.

The next room to consider is the living room. This can range from a small room around a fireplace to a Great Room that combines living room, family room, and dining area in one. The living room should be at least as large as the master bedroom, and larger if there is no family room. Decide what the living room will be used for. Do you entertain often? Do you need plenty of seating space or open space? How many people will normally use the room at one time? On special occasions? How frequent are these special occasions? Monthly? Once a year? What adjoining areas can also be utilized?

Some families prefer to have the living room for the adults and a family room for children—preferably at the other end of the house. However, families that do most of their activities together (TV watching, games, hobbies) find that either the living room or the family room never gets used. It's better to combine the rooms into one larger room than have one sit idle.

The kitchen is very important, especially to the cook. Although most homemakers don't spend as much time in the kitchen as those of previous generations, it is still a vital room. When designing your kitchen, review the uses of your current kitchen: baking, meal preparation, canning and freezing, clean-up. Do you need a kitchen with lots of counter space, or minimal counter space? We'll design your kitchen later, but for now, consider whether a large or small, separate or combined kitchen will best serve your needs.

Some homemakers prefer to combine the kitchen with the dining and/or family rooms. This is called a "country kitchen." It includes a bar, dining area, possibly a fireplace, and even a couch and chairs. This setup is perfect for families who do most activities together and do little formal entertaining. Otherwise, a separate dining room or dining area is preferred.

What other rooms would you include in your log home? By reviewing your family lifestyle, traffic, and needs, you may decide to add a study or home office near the quiet end of the home. You may include a pantry with storage for raw vegetables, canned goods, and

Fig. 3-4. The dining room can be an extension of the living room or a room by itself (courtesy New England Log Homes, Inc.).

Fig. 3-5. The kitchen reflects the mood of the entire home (courtesy New England Log Homes, Inc.).

a freezer. You could plan a large utility area, preferably near the back door, to serve as a "mud room," washing area, and storage room. You may want to include a small hobby room for setting up trains, building models, sewing, or playing games. You could have a "mother-in-law room" with cooking area and outside entrance. You may want to include a studio where natural light can come through skylights for painting or ceramics. You could add an indoor/outdoor room where children could play under shelter on rainy days. You could design an atrium in the center of the home for plants, or add a solar greenhouse to the side of the home near the kitchen for fresh vegetables throughout the year. Costs may eliminate some of these rooms later, but for now you can add on extra rooms in your imagination for free.

SIZING UP YOUR HOME

Once you've decided what rooms you'll need in your log home, you can begin sizing them for livability. For some people, an 8×10 foot bedroom is adequate while others can use nothing less than 14×20. The best place to start is again in your current home. Is your current master bedroom adequate in size for your needs? Do you plan to change or increase your furniture in your next home? If so, by how much? Will you be adding a larger dresser or chest? The majority of master bedrooms are between 150 and 200 square feet in size, such as 12×15. Children's bedrooms are often between 100 and 150 square feet; 10×12 is an example. Much depends on the number of people who will be using the room, the amount and type of furniture, and the availability of building funds. Bunk beds can stretch a smaller bedroom to comfortably sleep three, but some bedrooms can only house one teenager peacefully.

There's no such thing as the "typical size" bath. They can range in size from 5×6 feet (30 square feet) to 10×12 (120 square feet) or more. Much depends on your needs, the number and ages of family members, the number of baths in the home and—most important— your budget. The best way to size your bath is to look at the size of your current bath, those of friends and relatives, and those in log home catalogs. You may want to have one large bath with doors off two or more bedrooms (called a Continental bath) or two baths with separate basins and toilets sharing the bathtub.

As mentioned, living rooms come in all sizes and shapes depending on family needs and supporting rooms. In most homes the living room takes up about a quarter of the floor space. That is, a 1600 square foot home will have a living room of about 400 square feet, such as 16×25. In larger homes the ratio may go to 20 percent—520 square feet of living room in a 2600 square foot home.

If you want to sell your wife on this log home idea, mister, you'd better plan an efficient kitchen for her. The three major tasks performed in the kitchen (in case you haven't been in one for awhile) are storage and preparation, cleaning and dishwashing, and cooking and serving. The 1200 square foot home should have no less than seven feet of base cabinets. The 1600 square foot home needs eight feet or better and plan on nine feet of base cabinets for the 2000 square foot home. Add two feet for the sink and another two feet for the dishwasher to figure countertop area.

The work area can be any shape that's comfortable for the cook. The most efficient work area places stove, refrigerator, and sink no more than about five feet from each other. This can be done by bending the counters into an L or U, or by adding an island in the center of the U for homes with abundant countertop. Sometimes a break in the counter is necessary because of doorways or windows. Keep these to a minimum and eliminate through traffic in the kitchen for a happy homemaker.

Dining rooms are usually square and cover about the same floor space as the kitchen. They are usually adjacent to or part of the kitchen for efficiency. Review your lifestyle and frequency of entertaining to decide which type of dining area is most practical.

Laundry rooms need only be large enough for your washer and dryer (about ten square feet) plus a work area (from 12 to 20 square feet). Closets can be planned as the width of the room and to a depth of about two and a half feet. All bedrooms must have closets to be called a bedroom. Plan a hallway closet near the front door and a linen closet between the living area and the baths.

The family room, if included, is a variable. It can be as large as the living room or larger. Many families plan a smaller living room and enlarge the family area, depending on the number and ages of their children. Others simply put a common area between bedrooms for children to play in while they are young and plan to add an

Fig. 3-6. The location of a stairway is important to your log home design (courtesy Beaver Log Homes).

Table 3-1. Log Home Room Orientation by Region.

			Cool	Temperate	Hot-humid	Hot-arid
Living room	Orientation	Light	S.SE to SW	SE to W.SW	E.NE to NW	E.NE to NW
		Vent	Avoid winter winds.	Towards summer winds. Avoid winter winds.	Towards summer winds.	Towards summer winds.
		Humidity	Towards prevailing summer breezes.	Towards prevailing summer breezes.	Towards prevailing breezes.	Wind passage over water for cooling.
	Configuration	Light	E-W axis. Large openings. Close relationship to daily living spaces. Average ceiling height.	E-W axis. Large opening with capacity for summer shading. Close relationship to daily living spaces. Average ceiling height.	N-S axis or E-W axis with solar shading capability. Large opening if protected. Average otherwise. Open relationship to daily living spaces. High ceiling height.	N-S or E-W axis with thick thermal walls small opening high in wall. Close relationship to daily living spaces. Average ceiling height.
		Vent	Parallel axis to prevailing winds. Small openings. Compact plan. Average ceiling height.	Parallel axis to winter winds. Perpendicular axis to summer winds. Average opening. Compact plan. Average ceiling height.	Perpendicular to prevailing winds. Large opening. Open plan. High ceiling height.	Perpendicular to prevailing winds. Large openings. Open plan. High ceiling height.

Kitchen					
Orientation	Light	E.SE to W.NW	NW to E	NW to S.SE	NW to SE
	Vent	Towards summer wind.	Towards summer wind.	Towards summer wind.	Towards summer wind.
	Humidity		Towards summer wind.	Towards summer wind.	Towards prevailing.
Configuration	Light	N-S axis. Small opening. Kitchen should be centrally located. Average ceiling height.	N-S axis. Small opening. Kitchen should be centrally located. Average ceiling height.	E-W axis. Large openings. Kitchen to be located apart from daily living spaces to avoid heat transfer to those spaces. High ceiling height.	E-W axis. Large openings. Kitchen to be located apart from daily living spaces to avoid heat transfer to those spaces. High ceiling height.
	Vent	N-S axis. Compact layout. Low ceiling height.	E-W axis. Small opening. Compact layout. Average ceiling height.	NW-SE axis. Large openings. Open plan. Average ceiling height.	N-S axis. Large opening. Open plan. High ceiling height.

(courtesy Beaver Log Homes)

Table 3-1. Log Home Room Orientation by Region. (Continued from page 47.)

Bedroom			Cool	Temperate	Hot-humid	Hot-arid
Orientation		Light	NE to SE	NE to SE	NW to SE	NE to SE
		Vent	Protect from winter winds.	Protect from winter winds. Expose to summer breezes.	Orient to night breezes.	Orient to capture prevailing breezes.
Configuration		Light	N-S axis. Small opening. Separated from daily living spaces for privacy. Low ceiling height.	N-S axis. Small opening. Separated from daily living spaces for privacy. Low ceiling height.	N-S axis. Large opening. Separated from daily living spaces within open plan. Average ceiling height.	N-S axis. Medium opening. Separated from daily living spaces within compact plan. Low ceiling height.
		Vent	Parallel to prevailing winds. Small opening. Compact plan. Low ceiling height.	Parallel to winter wind. Perpendicular to summer breezes. Small openings. Compact plan. Low ceiling height.	Perpendicular to night breezes. Large opening. Open plan. Average ceiling height.	Perpendicular to prevailing winds. Small openings. Compact plan. Low ceiling height.

Bathroom		NW to E	NW to E	SW to NE	SW to NE
Orientation	Light				
	Vent			Avoid interference with prevailing winds.	Avoid interference with prevailing winds.
Configuration	Light	N-S axis. Small opening. Centrally located. Low ceiling height.	N-S axis. Small opening. Centrally located. Low ceiling height.	N-S axis. Medium opening. Separated from daily living spaces with access. Average ceiling height.	N-S axis. Small opening separated from daily living spaces with direct access. Low ceiling height.
	Vent	Parallel to prevailing winds. Small opening. Compact plan. Low ceiling height.	Parallel to prevailing winds. Small opening. Compact plan. Low ceiling height.	Perpendicular to prevailing winds. Medium opening. Open layout. Average ceiling height.	Perpendicular to prevailing winds. Medium opening. Compact plan. Low ceiling height.

Table 3-1. Log Home Room Orientation by Region. (Continued from page 49.)

		Cool	Temperate	Hot-humid	Hot-arid
Orientation	Light	SW to SE	W.SW to E.SE	SW to NE	NW to E
	Vent	Protected from prevailing winds.	Protected from winter winds.	Protected from winter winds and in direct path of summer wind.	Orient to capture and funnel prevailing winds through buildings.
Configuration	Light	Perpendicular to strongest sun. Large opening for solar heat gain. Vestibule space before entering living spaces.	Perpendicular to strongest sun. Large opening for solar heat gain. Vestibule space before entering living spaces.	Parallel to strongest sun. Average opening protected from sun. Direct entrance to living spaces.	Parallel to strongest sun. Small opening protected from sun Vestibule space before entering living space.
	Vent	Parallel to prevailing winds. Small opening. Compact plan.	Parallel to winter winds. Perpendicular to summer breezes. Small opening. Compact plan.	Perpendicular to prevailing winds. Large opening. Open layout.	Perpendicular to prevailing winds. Medium opening. Compact plan.
Entrance					

Storage			NW to NE	NW to NE	W to NE	S.SE to NW
	Orientation	Light				
		Vent	Exterior surface toward winter wind to act as buffer.	Toward winter wind to act as buffer. Avoid blocking summer breezes.	Orient to block winter wind and allow passage of summer breezes.	Avoid blocking summer breezes.
	Configuration	Light	Direct sun not needed. Small opening. Peripheral of living spaces. Low ceiling height.	Direct sun not needed. Small opening. Peripheral of living spaces. Low ceiling height.	Direct sun not needed. Average opening separated from daily living spaces. Average ceiling height.	Direct sun not needed. Small opening. Separated from daily living spaces. Low ceiling height.
		Vent	Perpendicular to prevailing winds to act as a buffer. Small opening. Compact plan.	Perpendicular to prevailing winds to act as a buffer. Small opening. Compact plan.	Parallel to prevailing winds to avoid blocking ventilation. Average opening. Open layout.	Parallel to prevailing winds to allow cool winds to strike the building. Small opening. Compact plan.

enclosing wall and doorway when they are grown and need their own private rooms.

Here are a few other things to consider as you design the rooms of your log home:

Exterior doors are usually 3'0" (36")×6'8". Plan the front door as close as possible to the garage, driveway, and major pathway. This prevents side doors from being overused and keeps guests from having to walk around your home to enter.

The standard windows are 2'8"×3'2" or 4'2". Stay with standard sizes if possible to reduce costs and make building your home easier. The so-called picture window which many like in the main room of a home is 4'×7'. Sliding glass doors are usually 80 inches high by five, six or eight feet wide.

Stairways should be 3'0" or 3'6" wide and eight to 12 feet long depending on how steep you want them. A spiral staircase, while attractive, is usually impractical. It takes up about as much floor space as a conventional stairway, yet cannot be used to move larger furniture to upstairs rooms.

A porch should have a northern or western exposure to keep it cool with air currents and give a place to watch the sunsets at the end of the day. A sunbather's porch should have (much like the bather) uncovered southern exposure.

Log homes with cathedral or open ceilings in the main living area often have a loft over the bedrooms or kitchen/dining area for extra sleeping space or storage. A simple pull-down stairway is all that's needed for access. Some builders provide loft access by building a ladder up one wall.

If you're planning an upstairs in your log home, you can do several things to increase your home's living area at a small increase in cost. Any upstairs space that's taller than 3'6" is considered usable living area. Though only small children could stand in an area this short, a knee-wall can be built under the roofline to this height and headboards and chests can be placed along these shorter walls. The roof's pitch will allow occupants to stand near the center of the room. You can add this partial second floor by simply adding a few extra rows of logs when you build. Another way is to increase the pitch of the roof. A third way is to add a partial or full dormer to the second story. If cost is a major consideration, a two-story home of 2000 square feet is less expensive to build than a one-story home of the same size.

Many architects suggest you build your garage on the west side of your home to block out the warm summer sun, but much depends on your local climate, the uses of your garage, and how well you

Fig. 3-7. Fireplaces should be in the center of your home for greatest heat efficiency (courtesy New England Log Homes, Inc.).

insulate your home. Patios should have a northern or eastern exposure, depending on how much sun you desire in the late afternoons and evenings when you will most use your patio.

Room orientation is a very important consideration in planning your home. A room that is positioned well for sun and wind can be a

Fig. 3-8. A dormer can turn a loft into a bedroom (courtesy Beaver Log Homes).

Table 3-2. Orienting Exterior Elements by Region.

Elements			Cool	Temperate	Hot-humid	Hot-arid
Paved areas		Sun	Use to reflect additional solar insolation to building and to form a warm air pocket.	Use to reflect additional solar insolation to building. Shade this area in summer to avoid heat build-up	Avoid excess build-up of solar insolation.	Avoid any reflection on building and additional heat gain.
		Wind	Place in direction of prevailing winds to carry any heat build-up to building.	Place in direction of prevailing winds to carry any heat build-up to building.	Avoid paved areas in path of summer winds.	Avoid paved areas in path of summer winds.
		Precipitation	Use for snow accumulation and additional reflection heat gain.	Use for snow accumulation and additional reflection heat gain. Use to improve drainage in summer.	Use to drain away any precipitation.	Use to collect rainwater for cooling.
Fences		Sun	Use to deflect prevailing winds. Avoid trapping cold winds.	Use to deflect winter winds. Use to channel summer breezes to the building.	Use to channel summer breezes to building.	Use to channel summer winds to the building. Use to trap any cold breezes.
Berms		Sun	Use to insulate building from cold temperatures.	Use to insulate building from cold temperatures.		Use to insulate building from hot temperatures.
		Wind	Use as a wind break from prevailing winds.	Use as a wind break in winter and to channel breezes to building in summer.	Use to direct wind to building.	Use to channel wind to building.

Elements						
Bodies of water	Sun	Preferred to south for additional reflection of solar insolation.	Preferred to south for additional reflection of solar insolation.	Avoid bodies of water to south and additional heat build-up.	Avoid bodies of water to south and additional heat build-up.
	Wind	Avoid bodies of water in path of prevailing winds.	Avoid bodies of water in path of winter winds. Preferred location of bodies in water in path of summer breezes.		Water preferred anywhere near building for cooling.
Rock formations	Sun	Preferred for solar reflection. Preferred near building to act as a thermal storage of heat. Avoid blocking path of sun.	Preferred for winter solar reflection and as a thermal storage of heat. Use to shade in summer.	Avoid increased heat build-up due to reflection. Use for summer shading.	Avoid increased heat build-up due to reflection. Use for shading. Use its thermal properties as a night time heat source.
	Wind	Use as a wind break.	Use as a wind break in winter and to channel winds to building in summer.	Avoid blocking prevailing winds. Use to channel winds to building.	Use to channel prevailing breezes to building.
Deciduous vegetation	Sun	Avoid blocking sun.	To south for summer shade.	To south for summer shade.	To south and west for midday and afternoon shade.
	Wind	Allow passage of summer breezes.	Channel summer breezes to building.	Use high canopy types to allow cooling breezes to strike building.	Channel winds to building.
Coniferous vegetation	Sun	Allow passage of sun.	Avoid placement to south.	Allow passage of sun.	Overhang building for shade.
	Wind	Use to protect building from prevailing winds.	Use to protect building from winter winds. Avoid blocking summer breezes.	Use to protect building from winter winds. Avoid blocking summer breezes.	Avoid blocking prevailing winds.

(courtesy Beaver Log Homes)

pleasure to use. It needs less heating and air conditioning to remain comfortable. Lighting costs are less and it's more natural. Tables 3-1 through 3-3 show how rooms should be oriented depending on your home's location (courtesy of Beaver Log Home). The best way to use these charts is to take a piece of paper, mark the points of the compass (North, South, East, West) on each side, find your local region on the map and draw each room separately, oriented as suggested. Where there are conflicts, choose the orientation of the room that's used the most—bedroom over utility, living room over bath.

SHAPING YOUR HOME

Designing your log home is much like making something with building blocks. First you choose what blocks you'll need (room selection), then you choose the sizes of your blocks (room sizing), then you begin positioning your blocks (room orientation), and finally you build your object (home shaping).

There are many shapes a home can take: long and narrow, square, L-shaped/single-story, one-and-a-half story, two-story, tri-level, and many others. The eventual shape of your log home depends on the number of rooms and their orientation, your budget, and your personal tastes. The most efficient design from both building and maintenance cost viewpoints is the square two-story home. However, many people prefer to trade some efficiency for convenience and build a rambling ranch-style home. That's where individual needs and tastes enter the design process.

For a young family, a two-story home may be most practical, giving the greatest space for the money while offering separation between the sleeping area upstairs and the living area downstairs. However, for a retired couple who don't need as much floor space and prefer everything on the same floor, a one-story home is ideal. Others will solve separation problems by having a T- or L-shaped single-story home.

The pitch or angle of the roof is an important design consideration for many reasons. First, the pitch of the roof is dictated by local weather. Homes in sunny, dry areas need only a minimum angle of pitch for the runoff of infrequent rain, while one in snow country will need a greater angle and more bracing to withstand heavy snows. Of course, the greater the pitch the higher the cost. But a greater pitch can also give you more room in your attic, loft, or second story.

Then there's style. Many log home builders fall in love with a particular style of home and design everything else—room number, size and placement—around it. There's nothing wrong with that. Of course, style modifications can be made to nearly any log home. A traditional ranch-style can be made to look like a "log cabin" with the addition of a full-width porch. A square two-story home becomes a colonial with tall pillars, a large front door, and a veranda. A plain log home can be dressed up with a Z-brace front door and window shutters. Landscaping helps, too.

One other design consideration perplexes many log home builders: How "authentic" do I want my home? Does it have to look like something Grandpa built with odd-size logs and white chinking or can it be built with uniformly milled timbers? Should I leave some of the bark on the logs or have them milled to the same diameter? The best answer is an individual one. Your tastes may be for modern furniture and conveniences, or they may be for rustic simplicity. What type of furniture do you prefer? Are you the pioneer type or the suburban type? Is your log home a weekend getaway from the sameness of the city or a retirement home where you can continue your previous lifestyle in a slightly more rustic setting?

CLIMATE AND ENERGY

One purpose of any home is to average out the variables of climate. We start a fire on a cool day and turn on the air conditioner when it's warm outside. You've learned that by orienting your rooms you can minimize these variables and reduce the costs of heating and cooling. But you still need energy.

You may have decided to rely heavily on solar, wind, water, and wood power. Or you may have found that man-produced power

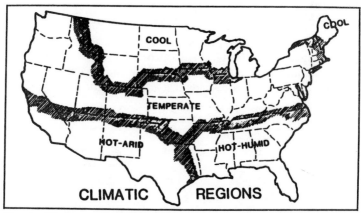

Fig. 3-9. Climatic regions of the United States (courtesy Beaver Log Homes).

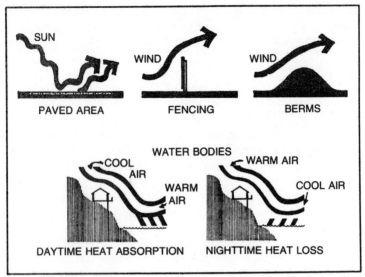

Fig. 3-10. Exterior elements affecting heating and cooling efficiency (courtesy Beaver Log Homes).

sources are more economical for you. The decision is based on what's available, the cost of installation, and the cost of use. Solar power is available to all sites, but the cost of installing adequate solar collectors in many northern climates may not be cost-effective. It may simply be cheaper in the long run to hook up to public power.

There are many ways to heat your log home. The most natural is wood heat. Most log homes are built in rural wooded settings where timber is plentiful at little or no cost. You can then heat your home with a wood stove or furnace placed centrally in the home, preferably in the main living area where it can be most effective and be tended. Common fireplaces, though romantic, are a poor and wasteful source of heat for any home. If you must have a fireplace, consider one of the new designs that are more efficient, or plan to use a fireplace insert.

Oil, gas, and electric heating can be used as a primary or secondary heating method depending on local availability and cost. Home designers today suggest you have at least two heating methods available to you such as electric heat and a wood stove, solar collectors and public power, or a furnace that can be converted to use either oil or wood fuels.

In temperate climates, the heat pump can be an efficient method of heating and cooling your home. The heat pump simply gathers and stores heat from the home for later discharge when it's needed. The heat pump equalizes temperatures in the home throughout the day without turning the furnace on and off or stoking the fire and later opening windows. Of course, nothing is free (or even cheap, anymore) and a typical heat pump system with ducting will cost $3000 to $5000 depending on the size of the home. Once installed, though, they cost less to operate than traditional heating systems.

Designing your home means not only planning rooms and heating, it also involves the installation of utilities. Because of the solidness of log walls, plumbing, wiring, and other utilities should be run through interior walls that are framed with dimensional lumber. Light switches are mounted more easily on interior walls. Bathroom plumbing should be routed through interior walls or fed through floors rather than through drilled logs. Upstairs plumbing and wiring should be right above downstairs utilities for greatest efficiency. Controls for rooftop solar collectors should be near the utility power box if possible.

SOLAR ENERGY

Increased emphasis is being placed on passive solar energy in

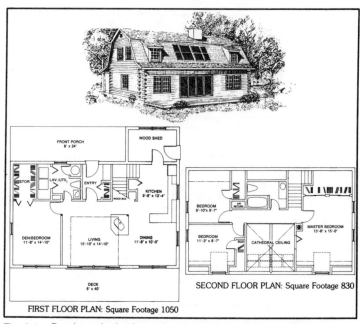

Fig. 3-11. Passive solar log home (courtesy Real Log Homes, Inc.).

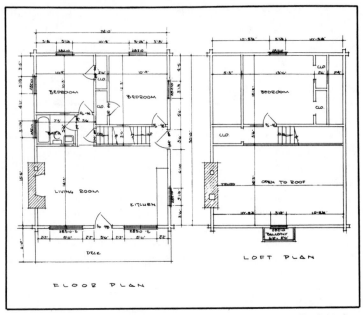

Fig. 3-12. Design your log home on paper (courtesy Northern Products Log Homes, Inc.).

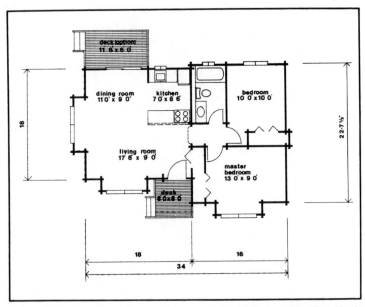

Fig. 3-13. Review floor plans of log home kits for ideas (courtesy Pan Abode Cedar Homes).

60

log home designs. Why? Because a passive solar system (one that uses design rather than equipment to take advantage of solar power) can meet about a third of the typical home's heating needs. That's substantial. In northern climates it reduces heating requirements by about 25 percent and by 50 percent or more in warmer climates.

There are three elements to any solar system, active or passive: *collection, storage* and *distribution*. The active system uses solar collectors to produce electricity that can be used within the home for many purposes. The passive solar system collects solar power with large, south-facing windows, skylights, and sliding glass doors. The heat is stored in energy walls and slabs. Distribution

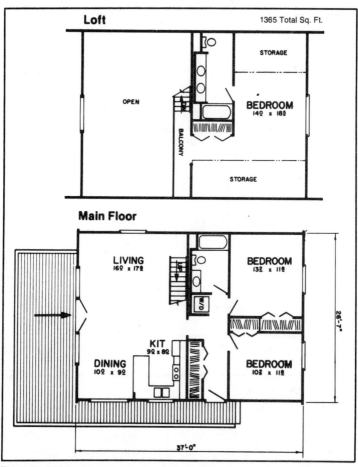

Fig. 3-14. This timber wall A-frame design is perfect for snow country (courtesy Justus Homes).

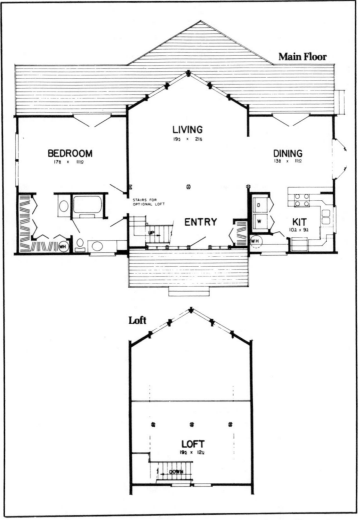

Fig. 3-15. A modern chalet-style timber home (courtesy Justus Homes).

comes from the radiation of the stored heat from walls and slabs into living areas as needed.

Of course, the design and building of a log home with passive solar resources is more costly than a conventional log home, but the investment can be cost-effective. If you are building your own log home, you may consider talking with a solar housing engineer or architect about design modifications to reduce heat loss. If you are planning on building a kit log home, you can talk with your dealer or

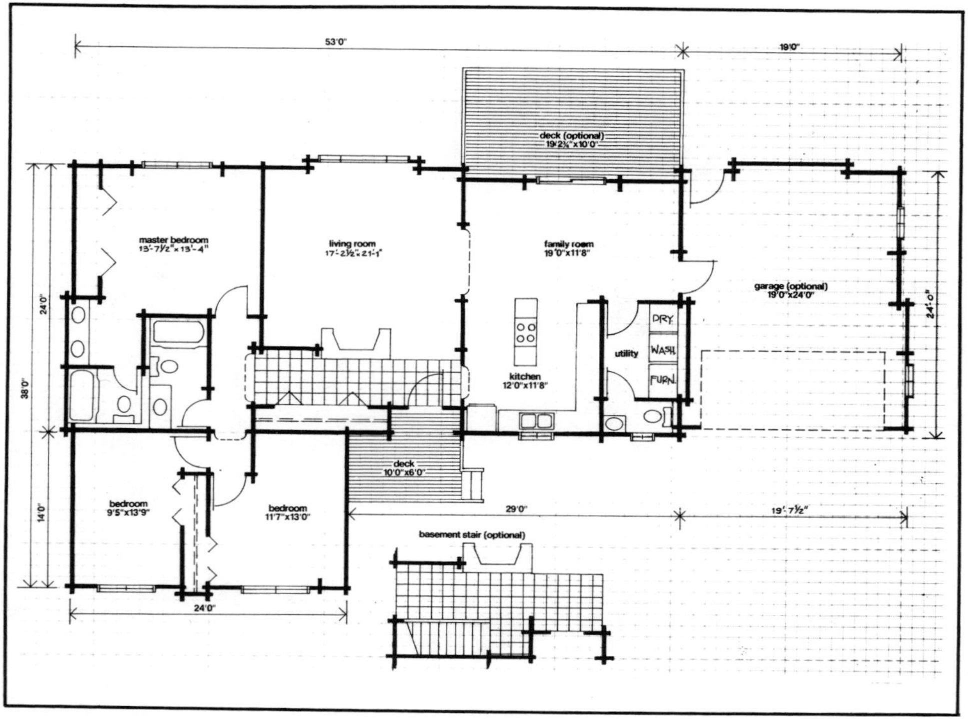

Fig. 3-16. A typical 1600 square foot home with three bedrooms, two baths, and a family room (courtesy Pan Abode Cedar Homes).

the manufacturer about passive solar designs they offer. There may even be some already erected in your region.

GETTING IT DOWN ON PAPER

You've considered just about every aspect of your home from size and shape to style and energy sources. It's time to get some of it down on paper. But rather than draw one perfect floor plan for your home, draw *four*. Make one a single-story log home, another a two-story home. Draw a "maximum house" and your "minimum house." Move rooms around. Consider alternative designs.

One of the greatest creative tools for the log home designer is the kit manufacturer's plan book. If you haven't sent for a dozen of them, do so. Addresses are in the back of this book. You'll find some unique design ideas that can be incorporated into your own custom log home—or you may find one that needs only one or two modifications to be your dream home. It's best to look at them *after* you've

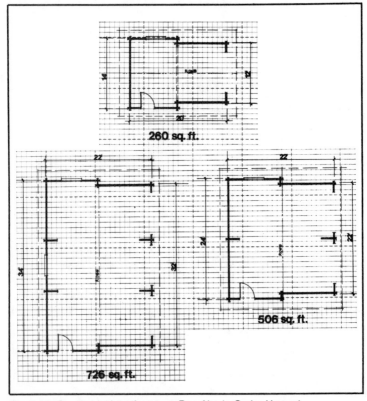

Fig. 3-17. Garage designs (courtesy Pan Abode Cedar Homes).

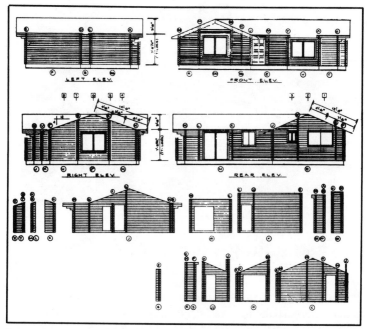

Fig. 3-18. A complete log home elevation diagram (courtesy Pan Abode Cedar Homes).

considered all the design elements in this chapter so that the home fits your desires rather than the other way around.

You may want to use the services of a log home architect—either an independent architect who has experience with log homes or the design department of one of the manufacturers. Why? Because building with logs has its own peculiar problems of load and stress, compaction, and shrinkage. Many architects aren't familiar with these. To find one, talk with other log home builders, write to manufacturers, and check ads in publications like the *Log Home Guide*.

Once you've settled on your design, you will have architect's drawings made up either by an architect or the manufacturer. The primary reason for a full set of plans is so that you, your contractor, and subcontractors (if any) know what you're doing. Another reason is for financing. If a banker is involved, he will insist on seeing full blueprints before the first dollar is spent. A third reason is that without complete and (almost) final plans, you can't estimate construction costs or get bids from the manufacturer, material sources, or subcontractors. You won't know how much this crazy dream is going to cost you. And that's the subject of the next chapter.

Chapter 4

Estimating Construction Costs

"Okay, so what's all this gunna cost me?" Cost is an important factor in planning and building your log home. You must know how much of your present and future assets you will have to trade for your home before you can decide to build it.

Actually, what you're searching for is *value*. You know about how much you can spend on your home: land, house, and amenities. What you *really* want to know is how much can you get for what you have. The problem is (if you're typical) that the home you've designed will cost about half again as much as you can afford. So you must cut costs where you can, primarily through smart shopping and reduced labor costs.

The purpose of this chapter is not only to show you how to estimate the cost of your log home, but also to show you how to get value from every dollar you spend.

There are two reasons why you need an accurate estimate of construction costs: budget and financing. Before you lay the first course of logs you must know whether you have enough money to complete your home. This takes a complete and detailed estimate. Also, if you are financing any part of your construction, you will have to furnish estimated costs to your lender. Bankers don't write blank checks.

There are three ways to estimate the cost of constructing your log home. The first is by square footage—that is, you can often get a rough estimate of construction costs by multiplying the square footage of your home by the local multiplier to come up with an approximate cost for the completed home as built by a contractor. An 1800 square foot home built in an area where custom frame homes cost about $40 a square foot (a figure available from local contractors) will cost about $72,000 plus land costs. You can save 20 to 50 percent by doing some or all of the labor yourself—and more if you supply the logs rather than buy them from a manufacturer.

Another way to estimate the cost of your log home is with percentages. The typical log home shell kit costs about 20 to 25 percent of the total cost of a completed log home. So you can multiply the shell price by four or five and get a rough idea of the cost at completion—again, if done by a contractor. Be careful, though. What one manufacturer calls a basic package may have little more than just the shell or exterior log walls. Decide what's included in the package before estimating costs based on the figures. More on this method of figuring costs later.

The third way is with an amplified estimate of costs broken down by components. That is, you develop estimates for the cost of site work, concrete/masonry, rough carpentry, roofing, electrical, finish carpentry, plumbing and heating. This can be done by getting bids from contractors and subs for both specific jobs and the entire construction project. Make sure they are familiar with log home construction and bidding. You can check many of the figures with the latest edition of *National Construction Estimator* published by Craftsman Book (542 Stevens Ave., Solana Beach, CA 92075). The *Estimator* will give you both material and labor costs for just about every building component as well as an index that will localize labor costs. It's written for frame construction, but can be easily modified for building log homes.

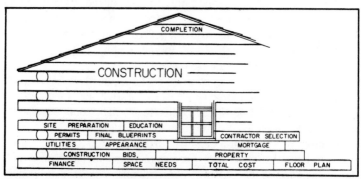

Fig. 4-1. The stages of constructing your log home (courtesy Authentic Homes Corp.).

Fig. 4-2. Full dormers can efficiently add size to your log home (courtesy New England Log Homes, Inc.).

Square foot and percentage estimates are excellent for telling you the approximate cost of your log home, but they are only *guidelines*. Before you turn the first spade of dirt or walk through your banker's door, you must have more accurate figures. Let's see how to get them.

AMPLIFIED ESTIMATE OF COSTS

Between 20 and 30 percent of the cost of your log home will be for the land on which it sits. The actual amount depends on how much land you purchased and the final price. You may have inherited 40 acres, or you may have to purchase your land at $5000 an acre.

A related cost is land preparation. This is where the do-it-yourselfer can save money because this job is labor-intensive. How much will you do yourself and how much will you hire done—and at what rate? Your site may need only to have bushes pulled up and removed or it may need 500 cubic yards or more of dirt removed before construction begins. You can get bids from contractors listed under "Excavating Contractors" in the Yellow Pages or in the Service Directory of area newspapers.

The septic system is another cost to consider. As ballpark figures, a 1000 gallon tank will cost about $600 installed, a 1250 gallon tank runs $750 and a 1500 gallon tank will be about $900 in the ground. Add on the cost of the drainfield: $1200 to $1500. A local contractor can give you a closer figure.

First-time builders often overshoot their budget because they didn't include *all* the costs of construction. Once the project is started, they find "nickel and dime" costs that increase the total costs by a few thousand dollars. One cost often missed in land preparation is survey fees. The typical two-man field party charges about $60 an hour to survey your land. A full survey will cost $150 to $300 or more depending on the size of the land and the number of angles. Don't forget the necessary local permits; they can add a few hundred more dollars to the cost.

Even if you're the rugged do-it-yourselfer who is going to cut down trees on your own property and haul them single-handedly to your building site, you should estimate the costs of construction. What tools are you going to need? A $250 chain saw? A winch? Special tools? Part-time labor? Most log home builders don't do everything themselves. They hire someone to cut the trees down, or haul them to the site, or help peel them. They may even purchase the logs pre-milled. The point is that whatever your method of construction, you must consider *all* the tasks involved and decide how much you are going to do yourself and how much you will hire done. Then you can estimate the costs of outside labor, tools, and materials.

If you are buying the logs from others (either on the stump or milled and delivered) you can get bids from suppliers by giving them your specifications and asking for a bid. To estimate the amount of logs you need, consider the height and width of each wall and the thickness of each log. Let's say you have a wall 30 foot long and eight feet high. The logs are 12 inches thick. That means you have eight rows (courses) of 30 foot logs (less any windows or doors). Eight times 30 equals 240 feet of 12 inch logs. Deduct the openings and you know how much you need. Total up all the walls, add logs used in the roof structure, porch construction, and any other structures (garage, shed, fencing). Put the facts down on paper and give them

Fig. 4-3. Stonework can add a great deal to the cost of your log home (courtesy New England Log Homes, Inc.).

69

Fig. 4-4. Building your log home on a slope may require more allowance for foundation costs (courtesy New England Log Homes, Inc.).

to suppliers with an estimated date of construction. If two suppliers have close bids, offer it to the one who will supply a better grade of log or will deliver the logs at no extra cost.

COMPARING KITS

If you've decided to build your log home from a manufactured

Table 4-1. Worksheet for Estimating Construction Costs.

Phase I — Foundation & subfloor	Land	$
	Permits & surveyor fees	$
	Land clearing, excavation & foundation	$
	Septic system & drains	$
	Materials for subfloor	$
	Labor for first floor	$
Phase II — Log package	Log package plus sales tax	$
	Transportation charges	$
	Labor for erecting log package	$
Phase III — Roof & 2nd fl.	Roofing/2nd floor materials	$
	Labor for roof & 2nd floor	$
Phase IV — Finishing & interior	Fireplace	$
	Rough stud carpentry	$
	Electrical	$
	Heating	$
	Plumbing	$
	Paneling & finishing materials	$
	Floor sanding and finishing	$
	Finish carpentry	$
	Cabinets	$
Phase V — Landscaping	Finish grading & landscaping	$
	Finished driveway	$
	Total	$

(courtesy New England Log Homes, Inc.)

Fig. 4-5. Under-porch storage space can reduce in-house storage needs (courtesy New England Log Homes, Inc.).

kit, be especially aware of what is and what *isn't* included in the package you order. As an example, one manufacturer offers a 1550 square foot kit at $12,800, while another sells a kit of the same size for $41,900. The difference is primarily in what's included in the "kit." The higher-priced kit includes doors, windows, roofing materials, closet materials, moulding, nails, and caulking. The basic kit only includes logs, sealer, and spikes.

As a rule of thumb you can usually multiply the cost of a shell kit by four to get an approximate cost as built by a contractor. A $15,000 shell kit will build a $60,000 home. Or you can add about 40 percent to the cost of the complete kit to estimate value. That is, a $43,000 full kit will build a $60,000 home.

Fig. 4-6. The cost of landscaping should also be considered in estimating construction costs (courtesy New England Log Homes, Inc.).

Fig. 4-7. Porches offer low-cost living space in temperate and warmer climates (courtesy New England Log Homes, Inc.).

To be more specific, you must break down the components of your planned kit and decide what else you will need to build it. Some manufacturers help this process by including a full materials list with the plans. Others offer optional packages you can purchase.

Another nickel-and-dime expense that can add to the cost of your home is transportation. A kit that takes two truckloads to be delivered from a factory 1000 miles away will add as much as $3000 to the cost of your home. The alternatives are to add this cost into the estimated price of any manufacturer's home, or to reduce the amount of material that comes from the factory—that is, buy what you can locally. Doors, windows, nails, flooring, and other stock materials may be less expensively purchased near your building site than imported.

As you estimate materials and labor needed to complete your log home, decide what's included in the kit. Are floor joists included? Sheathing? Framing and covering for interior walls? Insulation? Doors? Windows? Screens? Casings? Roofing? (What type?) Cathedral trusses? Cabinets? Countertops? Sinks? Plumbing? Wiring? Tub and shower enclosures? Mouldings? Door locks? Porch timbers? Stairs?

This is where a good contractor earns his money. He oversees the construction to make sure that all of everything is included in the bid sheet and ordered when it should be. The contractor usually gets about 15 percent of the total cost of the home—$9,000 for a $60,000

Fig. 4-8. Don't forget the cost of garages in your estimate (courtesy New England Log Homes, Inc.).

home—but can be a bargain for those without construction experience or log home builders who need financing. Most banks won't loan more than 50 percent of the construction costs to the do-it-yourself home builder.

OTHER CONSTRUCTION COSTS

Another forgotten cost in do-it-yourself home construction is that of utilities. For those building on subdivision lots it's simply a matter of running electrical, phone, and water lines a few dozen feet from the street to the house. But in rural construction, bringing utilities to the site can be expensive. The best way to get actual costs is to get bids from the appropriate utilities once you've chosen your site. Have them inspect the site to forsee any special problems that you can solve before construction begins. Get a written bid on installation and make sure all the facts are in writing: type of service, location of current service lines, site location, distance to

Fig. 4-9. Some families design expansion space, such as a rear wing, for future needs (courtesy New England Log Homes, Inc.).

Fig. 4-10. Compare kit costs, as some are less expensive than others (courtesy Beaver Log Homes).

be covered, cost per foot, ownership of the utility lines, easements, and lead time needed before construction. Then talk with neighbors about alternatives. You may be able to tap into an existing power line or draw from a neighboring well. You may discover that another landowner is interested in building nearby and may share costs with you.

Don't forget temporary power. You'll probably need at least electrical power on your site for saws, lighting, and other equipment. A typical drop pole and power box will run about $200 to $250 if power is nearby. You may also need water and sanitary facilities on-site.

Estimating the cost of your foundation is simple. Most foundation subcontractors will give you a ballpark figure over the phone unless you need a non-standard foundation wall. A simple foundation will cost about $1000 for the average home. The daylight basement foundation can run $3000 to $5000 depending on height, size, and thickness of the wall. For a closer bid, put your needs in writing and give it to Foundation Contractors listed in the phone book.

Fireplaces are more difficult to estimate due to their individuality. One log home owner may build a simple mantle-high used brick fireplace for a hundred dollars in materials while another may have a mason construct a two-story rock fireplace with a 48 inch box. As a starting point, you can estimate that a basic common brick fireplace will cost about $1000 installed and a fancy one will run to about $2000—and that is half labor and half for materials.

If you're planning other masonry work you can figure that the typical bricklayer or stone mason earns $15 to $20 an hour. If you decide to do your own masonry work, an excellent book on the subject is Charles R. Self's *The Brickworker's Bible* (TAB Book No. 1204).

Subflooring can be estimated at .85—$1 a square foot—that is $1275 to $1500 for a 1500 square foot single floor home. That includes 2″×10″ floor joists and ¾ CDX plyscore. Double that figure for the cost with a finished tongue-and-groove pine floor. The second floor can be built for about $1.50 a square foot including joists and finished T & G flooring. Of course, much depends on the grade of dimensional lumber, the source, and when you buy it. Add labor costs to these figures.

Carpeting is a variable. Prices can range from $10 to $30 a square yard installed. You can sometimes get a builder's discount from a carpet store even though you are a do-it-yourselfer. Or you can have a subcontractor bid it for you. Standard grade inlaid linoleum costs about half as much as carpeting.

When comparing the prices of flooring, remember that a square yard is *nine square feet*. Flooring that costs $12 a square yard is $1.34 a square foot. If T & G pine flooring is $1 a square foot, it's $9 a square yard—about 25 percent less than standard carpeting and half as much as good carpeting excluding labor. Of course, installation of a wood floor is more labor-intensive than carpet. The choice is pretty close. After reviewing the costs, you may decide to modify your home plans slightly one way or the other.

There's a great variation in the price of cabinets and the log home builder should price many models before choosing. The cabinetry in a simple kitchen can be purchased for $500 while the expansive kitchen with quality cabinets can be $2000 or more. Or the do-it-yourselfer can build his own cabinets with dimensional lumber purchased or cut for the cost of materials.

Fig. 4-11. The basic log home (courtesy Ward Cabin Co., Inc.).

Fig. 4-12. Initial and maintenance costs can be reduced through the selection of darker wood stains and preservatives (courtesy Ward Cabin Co., Inc.).

Don't forget to estimate the price of other cabinets through the home: bathroom, storage, garage, basement, and china. The *National Construction Estimator* can help.

HIRING A GENERAL CONTRACTOR

As noted earlier, you may decide to use the services of a general contractor to build your log home because of your lack of experience in construction or because the bank just won't finance your home without one. A well-chosen contractor can earn his fee by purchasing materials at discounts unavailable to you. And you can save money in constructing your home by hiring yourself back to the contractor at an agreed rate to assist him in building your home.

You may have trouble finding a general contractor who will work with you. Nothing personal, but few contractors have the knowledge and experience in log home construction it takes to make it profitable for them. Some would just as soon not mess with it. Besides, many contractors prefer not to build custom homes because the owner often wants to change things along the way—and most do. The only way many will do it is to be hired on a cost-plus basis—they earn a set percentage of the cost to construct the home.

There are a couple ways to solve the problems of experience and reluctance. If you are building your log home from a kit, you can purchase it from an experienced dealer/contractor and have him build some or all of it. Shop for the dealer as closely as you shop for your log home because a quality log home that's poorly constructed is less valuable than an economy home that's well built. As you talk with dealer/contractors, ask them for a list of the owners for whom they have built. Then contact these owners, asking about their experiences. Also ask if they know of any dissatisfied customer of this or any other dealer or contractor in the area.

If you're building your log home from scratch, you can hire an experienced scratch log home builder to be your contractor or supervisor. Experienced builders in your area are available by talking with log home building schools about alumni, from ads in log home publications like the *Log Home Guide*, with a Help Wanted ad in back-to-nature publications such as *Mother Earth News*, and by asking other log home owners in your area. In many rural areas you can come up with a crew of six or more experienced log home builders by simply asking around.

To get bids from contractors you must furnish them with building plans and information on the kit or logs you will use. They can then develop an estimate of construction costs for you, which you can double-check with the three methods of estimating costs outlined earlier in this chapter: square foot, percentage, amplified. Get more than one bid even if you're working primarily with a dealer/contractor. A second bid will keep him honest and help you decide whether you're getting your money's worth.

BE YOUR OWN CONTRACTOR

You may decide to become your own general contractor and supervisor. By doing so you can save about 15 percent on the cost of your home. If you are knowledgeable about home construction and aren't building a "problem home" you can often do as well as the typical contractor. What you lack in experience, you make up in enthusiasm and interest.

The first thing to do if you've decided to be your own contractor is to learn whether special licenses are needed in your area. The training and fees may prohibit you from getting the required license for the construction of just one home. And your banker may not give a construction loan to an owner/contractor. Check first.

Fig. 4-13. Many log home owners use their units primarily for recreation (courtesy Ward Cabin Co., Inc.).

Fig. 4-14. Finished A-frame home shown in floor plan in Fig. 3-14 (courtesy Justus Homes).

If you can and are willing to do it, begin your education by reading as much as you can about construction of log and frame homes. S. Blackwell Duncan's book, *How to Build Your Own Log Home & Cabin From Scratch* (TAB Book No. 1081) is a more technical book on log home construction written by an experienced builder. Another recommended title is *The Art of Log Building* by Manny Sievert (TAB Book No. 1342).

Subcontractors for electrical, plumbing, heating, cabinets, framing, sheetrock, and other jobs can be found through local trade unions, "Services" columns in the classified ads, and by asking around. Most can have a written bid for you within five working days.

You will also want general laborers for constructing log walls. They don't have to be experienced, but it is better to have at least one person on the site who has log wall construction experience. This may be the kit dealer, a subcontractor, a friend, or you. You may have volunteered to help someone else erect their log home for the experience and a few brews.

Authentic Log Homes has a valuable table for estimating the number of hours it will take to construct your log home shell:

Function	Man Hours Per Square Foot Of Floor
1 Sort and stack logs	.02
2 Erect first story logs	.04
3 Erect single story gables (2)	.02

Function	Man Hours Per Square Foot Of Floor
4 Log floor joist system	.02
5 Second story walls	.06
6 Second story gables (2)	.03
7 Gambrel gables	.04
8 Log rafter system (main)	.035
9 Log rafter system (porch)	.015

As an example, let's consider the approximate building time for their Oneida model, a ranch-style log home of 1383 square feet on one floor:

Function As Above	Man Hours	Building Hours With A Crew Of Five
1	27.66	5½
2	55.32	11
3	27.66	5½
4	not applicable	—
5	not applicable	—
6	not applicable	—
7	not applicable	—
8	48.41	9¾
9	20.75	4¼
Totals	179.80	36

That means a crew of five can build the shell of this home in about 36 working hours (about five days). Other jobs such as roofing, installing utilities, and framing the interior must be calculated separately. This can be done with your *Estimator* book and with bids from appropriate subcontractors.

FINANCING YOUR LOG HOME

Some log home builders will simply log trees off inherited property and build their log home right on the site. Chances are they will pay for hardware and tools and they won't have to borrow a dime. But the majority of log home builders must finance at least some of the costs of their homes: land, kit, materials, or the entire project.

With the cost of financing doubling in the last decade, you must be especially aware of how to get the greatest value for future dollars. You must understand the financial marketplace and know how to "shop smart." This aspect of building, more than any other, is where you can win or lose.

Fig. 4-15. Finished chalet-style timber home shown in floor plan in Fig. 3-15 (courtesy Justus Homes).

When you go for financing through a conventional lender—a bank or savings and loan—you'll need four things:

Complete building plans—No lenders are going to invest their depositors' money in a home that's drawn out on the back of a lunch bag. They want to know that the entire project has been thought out. They prefer to see professionally-drawn plans and often require a copy for their loan committee and files.

Complete cost estimates—Lenders will also want to know what the completed home will cost to build. They aren't interested in a guess of "somewhere around $40,000 to $50,000." They want written estimates and bids with specific amounts and how the totals were calculated. You may be able to do much of this yourself with subcontractor bids, the *National Construction Estimator*, and the help of your log kit manufacturer.

A general contractor—Most banks will work only through known general contractors, but because log home construction is a specialized field they may even want one with log construction experience. If you have some building experience or can get a general contractor's license in your area, you may be able to get financing through a bank. Start now by contacting loan officers personally about their requirements and possibly transferring your funds to a cooperative lender to build up credit and rapport. Otherwise, hire a general contractor.

A package—Bankers like professionalism. They not only want the facts, they want it presented as if you fully expect them to make the loan. Have information on your proposed home, your job and credit rating, your participation in the building of the home and any illustrations that will help the lender visualize your project. Have this information copied and put it in a neat folder to be left with the banker. Lenders like to be sold, too.

The best source of cooperative lenders is other log home owners. By now you've probably visited with many log home families in your area. Maybe you've asked them about their lender. Does one name come up more than others? If so, will some of these borrowers give you a letter of introduction to specific loan officers? The next best thing is to talk with primary lenders in your area about considering financing a log home. Some won't know what you're talking about, while others may be considering a log home themselves and may be very receptive.

The major sources of mortgage money today are savings and loan associations, commercial banks, mortgage companies, mortgage brokers, mutual savings banks, large credit unions, and private lenders. You can find them listed in your area Yellow Pages.

A so-called "conventional loan" is one that's taken through a conventional lender such as those just listed. The rate of interest is rarely negotiable; it's usually the rate publicized for the week the loan is approved by the lender. A typical conventional loan is for 80 percent of the value of the home. Sometimes a borrower can earn a lower interest rate by reducing the lender's risk with a larger down payment. However, lenders unfamiliar with log home construction may ask for a larger owner equity anyway.

Log homes have also been financed with FHA (Federal Housing Administration) and VA (Veterans Administration) guaranteed loans. These agencies guarantee the top 25 percent of the loan. This insurance is paid for by the borrower in the case of an FHA loan (½ percent of the loan amount) or by the government with a VA loan. There are also private mortgage insurance companies that can insure loans for 90 and even 95 percent of the home's value. Again, you will have to shop around before finding a willing lender.

Most lenders won't pay you or your contractor all the money you need in cash, but will write a "construction loan" for a specific time such as six months and give you the money in phases. A typical construction loan will be paid in five payments as each of five phases of construction are completed. When the home is done, the construction loan will be paid off by a conventional mortgage loan which will stay with your home 30 years or until paid off.

There are other ways of financing your log home. They are called "creative financing techniques." Here are a few:

Mortgage other assets. If you own other assets, real property, rentals, a boat, cars, stocks, or leases, you can sometimes use their value as collateral for a loan that will not attach your log home. Or you can use them as additional collateral to lower the bank's risk and get you a loan where doors were closed. If you own the property on which you are building, it can serve as collateral for your loan. If you are still buying the land you can sometimes get the seller to "subordinate" his interest—that is, let a lender have the first mortgage on the property and he take second position. Why should he? Because second position on a loan against land *and* a home is better than first position against just land. Talk to your lender about this.

Private lenders. There are many people with cash in the bank who would prefer to loan it directly to borrowers and earn a higher interest than banks pay. Some are looking for mortgages—first and second. You can find these private lenders directly through ads in the financial section of your newspaper or indirectly through mortgage brokers. The mortgage broker simply acts as an agent for private lenders and earns his fee by finding people who want to borrow money for secured purchases.

Friends and relatives. Many do-it-yourself builders who can't get full mortgages can find lenders in their own circle of family and friends. Ask around. Some may be private lenders looking for a better investment. *Warning:* Make your dealings businesslike and separate from any other relationships.

You've got the money you need, now let's get building!

Chapter 5

Your Building Site

Where you build can be as important as *what* you build. Your building site will be dictated by a number of factors, perhaps the greatest being its proximity to jobs in your field or, if you're retired, weather and recreational opportunities. Other practical considerations include the availability of public and private utilities, water and drainage, view, exposure, and site accessibility.

So take a careful look at where you build first to minimize problems. If you haven't chosen your building site yet, this chapter can guide you. If you already have your land, this chapter can help you choose your specific site and develop it with the fewest problems. You'll also learn how to prepare your building site for construction.

The first step in your search for the ultimate building site is to decide what you're looking for—and why. Somehow, you're going to have to narrow the search down from the more than two billion acres of land in the United States and nearly two and a half billion acres in Canada! The initial question is: How much land do you need and why?

Because of job and other commitments you may desire nothing more than a large lot in a tranquil subdivision near a metropolitan area. Many log homes are built on just such lots across the country.

You may need a large piece of farm land to start or continue an agri-business raising crops for sale. The type of farm you need will often dictate the minimum size and even the area.

Your plans may be for a working ranch where animals are raised for sale: cattle, horses, pigs, chickens, turkeys, etc. Again, use will dictate size. A cattle ranch requires hundreds of acres to be a full-time business, while a chicken ranch can be profitable on less than five acres.

You may want to be a tree farmer, growing and harvesting trees for sale. You'll need both size and an inventory. Even Christmas trees can't be harvested for four to six years. Commercial timber takes half a century or more. You'll need a large parcel with marketable timber already on it.

You may be planning to build your log home on enough land for you to become self-sufficient, raising your own food and a small cash crop. If you've researched this possibility you know how much land you'll need and what type of soil and climate is preferred. It can be anything from a couple acres to 20 acres or more.

Or maybe you're retired and your main purpose for your log home is to offer shelter with a view. You want to live on top of the mountain, at the sea, or near a river. Again, you must decide where and why.

Land is priced by the law of supply and demand. That is, if the supply is short and the demand is great, prices are high. Where land is plentiful and demand is low, prices are lower. What makes the supply and demand change? Isn't the supply of land great? Yes, but not where most people decide to live. There are more than four and a half billion acres of land in North America, *but* the majority of the population lives on a few hundred thousand acres clustered into major metropolitan areas. They live there to be closer to jobs, services, and conveniences. When jobs were on the farm, the rural areas were more populated and a smaller segment of the population lived in the city. Now the demand for space is where the supply is least, so making prices higher. In fact, in major cities, some land is sold by the *square foot* because of low supply and high demand.

What this law of supply and demand tells you is that the closer you build to where *others* live (to be near jobs or special amenities), the greater the cost of land. You may decide that the price is worth the value or you may decide it isn't. In either case, this principle affects the price you pay for land.

Another factor in the cost of land is *anticipated growth*. That is, a rural parcel that's expected to become surburban within the next decade or two will have a higher price tag than one that will remain rural. If you're looking for growth, you may want to purchase this parcel in the path of progress. If you're searching for privacy you may decide to stay away from anticipated growth properties. How?

You can mark growth areas out in any community by studying its road system on a map. Where major roads converge you can expect the first growth—the larger the road, the greater the chances of growth. Roads between communities also draw growth. Farming areas away from major roads are the slowest to change. Woodlands away from utility sources also grow slowly, but you must check the ownership and use of neighboring lands to make sure the areas won't soon be logged off and developed.

There's one other condition that affects the price of land: terms. Cash buyers usually get the best price. The land buyer who puts 25 to 50 percent down gets a price only slightly higher than the cash buyer. But the buyer with just 5 or 10 percent down is a risk to the seller and the price is higher. He may pay half-again as much as the cash buyer—*plus* interest.

You can use these facts of land pricing to get yourself the best deal in purchasing your log home site.

CHOOSING YOUR LAND

By now you've narrowed down your search for land to a specific area because of jobs, size and type of land available, view, recreation facilities, and available cash. Now it's time to begin your search for a specific parcel that will best fit your needs and limitations.

Many land buyers begin with a local real estate agent who is experienced in buying and selling the type of property you want. Agents, like most professionals, soon specialize—some in commercial properties, some in income properties, others in residential homes, a few in agricultural parcels. The one who specializes in the type of property you want to buy will be more efficient than a general real estate agent. Also, one who is a member of a local Multiple Listing Service can show you properties listed by other brokers in the area.

Or you can work direct with land owners who have property available. If you have experience in real estate purchasing you can often save the agent's commission by dealing direct. However, in many cases this is false economy if there are problems of title or contract terms.

Local climate is a consideration in purchasing land. Even though you have chosen to live in a general climatic region (cool, temperate, hot-arid or hot-humid) your area may have its own unique weather. One example is on the wet Olympic Peninsula of the Washington coast where some locations receive 100 inches of rain a year, yet miles away is a weather pocket around the town of Sequim where only 15 inches of rain is average. Some parts of the

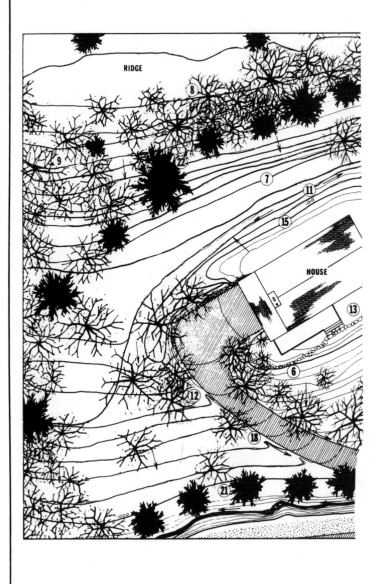

Fig. 5-1. Orienting your building site (courtesy Northern Products Log Homes Inc.).

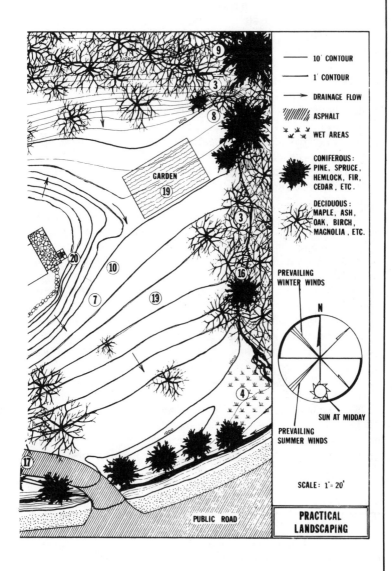

———————	10′ CONTOUR
———————	1′ CONTOUR
⟶	DRAINAGE FLOW
▨	ASPHALT
⁂	WET AREAS
●	CONIFEROUS: PINE, SPRUCE, HEMLOCK, FIR, CEDAR, ETC.
❋	DECIDUOUS: MAPLE, ASH, OAK, BIRCH, MAGNOLIA, ETC.

GARDEN
⑲

⑨
③
⑧

③

⑳
⑯
⑩
⑦ ⑬

④

⑰

PUBLIC ROAD

PREVAILING WINTER WINDS

N

SUN AT MIDDAY

PREVAILING SUMMER WINDS

SCALE: 1′ = 20′

PRACTICAL LANDSCAPING

same county may receive drastically different weather. The "locals" can tell you about these variable conditions.

The parcel you choose must be accessible. *How* accessible depends on your needs. You may have a home business that requires you build your log home along a major road. Or you may only need a mailbox to earn your living. If you must commute daily, you need to know the distance to your job as well as year-round weather conditions that may affect your getting out. Will you be snowed in each year? Does that bridge below you wash out each spring? And if you're considering the possibility of selling your log home someday, decide whether it is in a location that will help it sell. Your final location will be a compromise of factors.

Topography is the physical features of land. The topography of one parcel may be mountainous while another is level. The topography is important because it somewhat dictates the use of the land. Level land can become farm land. Mountainous land becomes view property.

The log home is adaptable to level sites, mild sloping sites, or even steep hillsides. However, the primary use of the land may dictate the topography of your building site. If you're farming, you'll build at one corner of a level parcel. If you desire a view, you may build on the side of a slope. If your purpose is self-sufficiency, you may want to build on a south-facing slope near level ground where crops and animals can be raised.

As you plan around topography, disturb as few natural contours as possible. Unnecessary shifting of earth causes erosion, destruction of soil structure, root systems, nutrients, and the natural compaction/aeration balance.

The availability of water supply, electricity, gas, and sewage disposal is an important consideration in the selection of your parcel and eventual building site. If a septic system is required, a percolation test—"perc test"—should be made before the land is purchased. You can do it yourself or have it done by an experienced tester who may be able to spot the best site using his knowledge of local conditions.

If you are using a spring-fed water system, have the potability of the water tested before buying a parcel. A local well driller can give you a general idea of the depth and quality of wells near your parcel before you buy.

If you're planning on running public utilities into the property, check with the companies first for a bid on how much it will cost. This can make a difference in the relative costs of properties you are considering.

The cost of owning property is more than just the cost of land. It also includes the price of amenities that make it liveable: utilities, services, roads, and taxes. Property taxes on land in the Ozarks can be as little as $10 to $25 a year while taxes on a similar parcel in another area may be $1000 a year or more. As you search for land for your log home, check with local officials to learn what the tax structure is in the area *and* whether it's expected to change in the next few years.

Minimal taxes mean minimal public services, so you may prefer to live in an area where taxes are higher to take advantage of better schools, roads, and recreation. In fact, if you have or expect to have school-aged children, one consideration in land selection will be the local schools. How are they rated against the national average? State averages? Regional averages? Are changes expected because of an influx of new residents or the planned shutdown of a major employer? How are local schools funded? How much is federal money, state money and local tax money? The greatest funders have the greatest control.

Commercial services are yet another consideration. Where will you do your primary shopping? How much and how often? If you are self-sufficient, the commercial services don't have to be as convenient as when you rely entirely on them. Some "hermits" reduce their dependence on stationary commercial services even more by doing their primary shopping through the mails.

One other thing: Check into the structure of the local government before your purchase property within a jurisdiction. Some governments will leave you alone and let you build how and where you see fit. Others won't allow you to put up a fence without a permit and inspection. Neighboring counties can be very different (and often are) in their governmental philosophies.

PLANNING YOUR BUILDING SITE

Okay, you've purchased your land and you're ready to start laying it out so you can begin building. The first thing you'll need is a detailed plot map. Chances are you had a survey made of the property when you bought it. A map of the property was also included in the title report you received when the transaction was closed. Using this map, you can draw out the proposed location of your log home, other use areas, driveway, utilities, and roads.

Your first task is to choose the most appropriate building site. Your first four considerations in orienting the home are: sun, wind, weather and view. Let's look at them one at a time:

Sun—You basically want a site exposed to the sunshine for direct solar gain, but sheltered from storms and cold winds. But you don't want the house so tightly surrounded by foliage that the sun never heats the house and the ground around it. Actual orientation

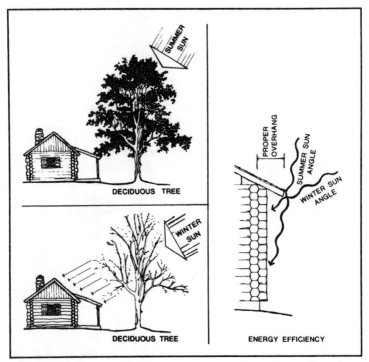

Fig. 5-2. If possible, deciduous trees should be on the south side of your home (courtesy Beaver Log Homes).

for maximum solar energy depends on the climate and the shape of the home.

Wind—The wind can be your greatest friend or worst enemy, depending upon how you use it. You can orient your home to protect it from prevailing winds while using the cooling breezes to your advantage.

Weather—Orientation of your home can also shelter it from adverse weather and even change weather conditions nearby.

View—Orientation can also increase the view from the primary living area of your home, but is often the least important consideration in how you place your home on your building site.

Table 5-1 shows you how to orient your home depending on whether your site is flat or sloped and based on your climatic region. As an example, your log home built on a sloped site in a cool region should be facing the south or southeast for the greatest sun and in a low position for wind shelter.

A *cool* region is one where the winters are very cold. Summer temperatures range from 10° to 90° Fahrenheit with less radiation

Table 5-1. Site Development Checklist.

			Cool	Temperate	Hot humid	Hot arid
Site orientation	Flat site	Sun	Southeast	South to Southeast	South	South
		Wind	Sheltered from North and West	Avoid exposure to winter winds. Expose to summer winds.	Sheltered from Northwest - open to prevailing summer breezes.	Expose to prevailing winds
	Sloped site	Precipitation	Near large body of water. Allow build-up of snow.	Close to water but avoid coastal fog. Allow build-up of snow.	Near any water	Near any water
		Sun	South or Southeast	South or Southeast	South	East to Southeast
		Wind	Low position for wind shelter.	Low position for wind shelter.	High position to catch wind	Low position for cold air flow.

(courtesy Beaver Log Homes)

91

Fig. 5-3. You can use a natural slope to your advantage by planning some living space in a basement (courtesy Ward Cabin Co., Inc.).

than the rest of the country. Winds are persistent, generally out of the northwest or southeast.

A *temperate* region is one with hot summers and cold winters. Considerable precipitation and high humidity cause prolonged periods of cloudy overcast days.

A *hot-humid* region has high temperatures and high humidity. Wind direction varies drastically. Hurricanes and tropical storms are common.

A *hot-arid* region has long periods of clear skies and a predominantly dry atmosphere. Winds are easterly or westerly.

Even the shape of your home affects its preferred orientation. As you can see in Table 5-2, a rectangular home will be oriented differently than a square home to take advantage of the sun and wind

Fig. 5-4. Building on a berm can give you additional basement access (courtesy Ward Cabin Co., Inc.).

Table 5-2. Home Orientation by Building Shape and Region.

		Cool	Temperate	Hot-humid	Hot-arid
	Sun	Orient E-W so long side is toward sun.	Orient E-W so long side is toward sun.	Orient N-S to E-W to receive maximum morning sun and minimum noon and afternoon sun.	Orient N-S to E-W to receive maximum morning sun and minimum noon and afternoon sun.
	Wind	Orient point of building toward prevailing winds for deflection of wind and protection of front of building.	Orient point of building toward prevailing winds for deflection of wind and protection of front of building	Orient long surface perpendicular toward prevailing wind for cooling.	Orient long surface perpendicular toward prevailing wind for cooling.
	Sun	Orient to create a heat trap.	Orient to create a heat trap.	Orient so as not to form a heat trap.	Orient so as not to form a heat trap.
	Wind	Protect interior court from prevailing winds.	Protect interior court from prevailing winds.	Capture prevailing winds with interior court for cooling.	Capture prevailing winds with interior court for cooling.
	Sun	Orient NW-SE so all sides receive sun.	Orient NW-SE so all sides receive sun.	Orient E-W to free a facade from receiving direct sun.	Orient E-W to free a facade from receiving direct sun.
	Wind	Orient point of cube toward prevailing winds to deflect the wind and protect the front of the building.	Orient point of cube toward prevailing winds to deflect the wind and protect the front of the building.	Orient flat surface perpendicular to prevailing wind for cooling.	Orient flat surface perpendicular to prevailing wind for cooling.

(courtesy Beaver Log Homes)

Fig. 5-5. Site your home for the greatest protected view (courtesy Ward Cabin Co., Inc.).

in each region. An L-shaped log home in a cool climate will be oriented to create a heat trap while siting it to protect the interior court from prevailing winds. The idea is to gather and hold any solar heat available to increase comfort and reduce energy costs.

Another consideration in siting your home is how and where to install your driveway. Don't place a driveway directly down a slope. Curve the road down slopes to prevent rapid, damaging water runoff. Steeply-sloped driveways can also be hazardous during icy conditions. *Crown* your driveway—that is, make the center higher than the sides—and provide drainage ditches on both sides to prevent washouts. Drainage ditches are especially important on the downhill side of the driveway where surface waters collect. To improve existing ditches on the downhill side, line them with large flat stones or asphalt and reinforce them with a short bank beyond the ditch. Standing water on a driveway can be a hazard, especially during the winter months.

Access to your building site may be across property owned by someone else who has given you the right of *easement*, or the right to pass. Make sure this easement is in writing and recorded in the county courthouse. A handshake is fine for the two of you, but if either party sells his property the new owner may not understand or honor your verbal agreement. Also, if an easement gives a number of landowners the right to pass, make sure you have a common road agreement written and recorded. Decide how the road to your homes will be maintained and how the costs will be divided—by property size, value, or other measurement. If many people use the road you may want to talk with the county about vacating the road, deeding it to them for public ownership and maintenance. You may have trouble getting them to take it over unless you can prove that it's in the general public's interest.

If you must build your log home near a public road, you can reduce heat, dust, and noise by planting a dense hedge or row of evergreens along the road. This will also improve privacy.

PREPARING YOUR BUILDING SITE

The idea behind clearing land for a building site is to remove all objects from where the home will sit without destroying everything around it. The rocks, trees, and brush left intact can be used to prevent soil erosion and become natural landscaping for your site. However, you may need to change the grade of your site slightly to encourage proper drainage.

Trees play an important role in Nature's climatic control. Retain as many naturally occurring trees as possible. This controls erosion, retains the established root systems, cuts glare, and provides shade. Naturally occurring trees are the hardiest for your area, so if you plant new trees, prefer the same species. When selecting trees to remain on the site, look for those that are healthy, vigorous, and have well-formed crowns. A healthy crown should make up at least 30 percent of the total height of the tree. Tall, spindly trees with a small live crown could be unhealthy, subject to wind-throw, and more susceptible to insects and disease.

When excavating the building site with heavy equipment, take care to prevent damaging the trees you retain. Trees can easily be

Fig. 5-6. Efficient site planning yielded twice as much livable space in this log home (courtesy New England Log Homes, Inc.).

damaged by uncovering the roots or scraping their bark during excavation. This type of damage will permit disease and insects to penetrate the trees and possibly result in their eventual death. Another type of tree damage created during excavation is caused by piling dirt too closely to the base of the tree, covering the air roots and slowly suffocating it.

If solar heating units are planned, cut back or eliminate trees on the southern side of your house that are higher than 33 degrees from horizontal.

When grading your site, disturb the fewest natural contours possible. Slope the ground away from the house for at least ten feet for drainage, but don't drop elevations drastically around the building if possible. A gentle slope is best for adequate drainage without erosion.

Once grading is done, mark out your building site with stakes to ensure that it's positioned properly. We'll cover excavating for the foundation in Chapter 7.

There's one more thing that you can do to prepare your home site for building: Exterminate the ground. You can reduce the chances of insect infestation of logs and other wood by spraying the area with professional-strength insecticide. A local garden shop or hardware store can recommend a brand and method of application. Or have the area professionally exterminated. In areas of heavy foliage where berries and other plants will soon take over bare ground, you may also want to apply a defoliant.

The ground is prepared, utilities have been trenched and installed, building permits have been secured, your logs are either at the site or on the way. The next step is to gather both men and materials together in preparation for the day you lay your first course of logs.

Chapter 6

Gathering Materials and Labor

The first step in putting a jigsaw puzzle together is sorting out the pieces. It's the same with constructing a log home. Before you begin building you must make sure you have adequate logs, finish materials, tools, and labor. The better you plan, the easier it will go together.

If you've cut and prepared your own logs right on the property, your initial problem of securing and transporting them is solved. However, if you have them milled off-site or purchase a log home kit, you still need to order them and plan delivery.

Most manufacturers require a deposit of 20 percent with your order and another 30 percent about 30 days before delivery. Then on or before delivery day, you must have the bill completely paid. Most purchasers prefer to the make the final installment after they have received and inspected the materials. They make it by certified check to the driver, factory representative, or dealer. We'll talk about how to check out the load as it arrives in Chapter 9.

Just as important is coordinating the arrival and storage of other materials—dimensional lumber, windows, doors, hardware, utilities, and cabinets. For this you need either a construction schedule or a place to store materials out of the weather until they are needed. If you're using a contractor, he will do the ordering by a planned construction schedule.

As you purchase these items not supplied by the kit manufacturer, make arrangements for delivery. Many building material

Fig. 6-1. Basic log home construction tools (courtesy New England Log Homes, Inc.).

firms will hold your order up to three months for delivery with a substantial deposit. In fact, if you order most of your materials through the same supplier, he may loan you warehouse space for materials and deliver them with just a couple days notice. These services can be worth hundreds of dollars, but you may have to shop around to find them.

To help you in your shopping, here are some standards for dimensional lumber used by many builders. The lumber standard is American Softwood Lumber Standard PS 20 (U.S. Dept. of Commerce), S4S with 19% moisture at the time of dressing. Structural framing (2×4s and larger) is No. 2 grade Douglas Fir or Southern Pine. Stress grade is 1750 psi minimum for all non-vertical framing and 1200 psi minimum for all other members. Plywood standard is Softwood Plywood—Construction and Industrial PS 1 (U.S. Dept. of Commerce) with DFPA grade-trademarks. Actual grades of plywood vary with use.

Pre-hung doors (those with casing and hinges) are the most popular. Exterior doors are usually 36 inches wide plus casings. Interior doors range from 30 to 36 inches wide. Solid pine doors are popular because of their lightweight and natural wood finish. Of course, they are also more expensive than the standard hollow door used in most frame construction. Make sure all doors match or surpass local building codes. Some codes require wood core fire doors in certain installations.

Windows are a matter of taste, efficiency, and economy. The most efficient windows are triple-pane with three layers of glass insulated by two air pockets. They are often as heat-efficient as the wall around them. Double-pane glass is next best and single-pane windows are energy wasters. Stay with standard sizes measured in six inch increments such as 3'0" × 4'6". The most common brands used in log homes are Anderson, Pella and Crestline, though you may find windows of regional manufacture that will work just as well. If you're cost-conscious, consider reducing the number and increasing the quality of windows in your log home. Installation of windows and doors will be covered in Chapter 11.

Most log building tools are basic construction tools such as hammers, saws, levels, tapes, caulking guns, and drills. The only one you wouldn't use to build a frame house is a chain saw. There are a number of ways to collect the tools you need in construction. You may have some of them in our own toolbox. If not, ask among your crew and friends (make sure you mark any borrowed tools with the owner's name; a grease pencil makes a good temporary marker). You may be able to rent some of the larger and more costly items including the chain saw. However, most log homes are built in areas where a chain saw is an important tool. You may as well go ahead and buy one.

In choosing a chain saw, you want power and versatility. An electric chain saw with a ten inch bar is limited to kindling and soft

Fig. 6-2. Most log home manufacturers have dealers of factory representatives who can help you gather men and materials (courtesy New England Log Homes, Inc.).

woods. If you're buying a long-term saw that you can use for log home construction, cutting firewood, and clearing your building site, you will want a heavy-duty saw with a 16 inch bar. The cost will be $250 to $400 new. As with any big-ticket item, shop around and talk with owners before you buy. *Don't* buy it at a discount store. Make sure parts and service are available, just in case.

The materials are on-site or ready for delivery, and your tools have been selected. Now you need labor. If you have a general contractor overseeing your construction, this problem is solved. He will hire laborers and carpenters to build the log walls and finish your home. If you are acting as your own contractor you'll have to do this yourself.

As mentioned earlier, labor for wall erection can be found anywhere. It takes no special skills—just strength. How much strength depends on the size and type of log you're using. Scratch builders often use logs of 15 to 20 feet or more, weighing hundreds of pounds. Kit logs come in shorter lengths for manufacturing and transportation economy and can usually be handled by two or three healthy men or women. Your labor force can be drawn from friends and relatives, other log home builders in the area, local employment offices, area colleges, and even construction sites where laborers are willing to work a couple weekends for cash.

Supervision may be offered by a factory representative or kit dealer, an experienced log home builder, or a friend in construction. If it comes down to you, make sure that you fully understand the steps of construction, have read and reread the construction manual and this book, and have visualized the steps in your mind. Then delegate before you start. Who will carry? Who will place? Who will spike? Who will seal? Who oversees? Who's in charge of refreshments?

With pre-planning, even inexperienced builders can erect a log home safely and efficiently.

Chapter 7

Excavating and Laying Your Foundation

Many old log homes are no longer standing—not through any fault of the logs, but because the foundation was inadequate. Built on wood or stacked rock fundations, these log homes were subject to insects, dry rot and the movements of the earth below. A poor foundation drastically shortened their lives.

A well-planned and constructed foundation can extend the life of logs by reducing exposure to moisture and changes in the earth. Because your log home is a large and long-term investment, you want to make sure its foundation is adequate to both support the weight and protect the components.

In this chapter you'll learn the what, why and how of foundations, and you'll learn that they're not as difficult to build as many imagine. The components are few and design help is available. Kit manufacturers supply information on foundation construction with their plans. Do-it-yourself builders can use a foundation contractor or design their own foundation with some basics and a few formulas.

FOUNDATION LAYOUT

The first step in planning and pouring your foundation is laying it out on the ground. This is usually done with what's called a "batter board" layout. The batter boards are two boards at right angles to each other placed at each corner of the proposed foundation, usually a couple feet out from the foundation line. Then strings are run above the foundation line from batter board to batter board. A rock

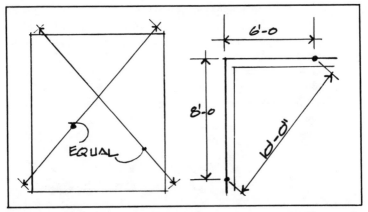

Fig. 7-1. When setting footing lines or stem wall forms, check all corners for square. This can be done either by measuring the diagonals of a rectangular foundation or measuring out from a corner six feet on one wall and eight feet on the other. The distance between these points should be exactly ten feet (courtesy Beaver Log Homes).

or other weight tied to the ends of the strings will hold them in place while still being movable.

Once the boards and strings are up, the builder checks and double-checks the squareness of the foundation strings and lengths of the proposed walls. A foundation that's two inches off or out of square can cause dozens of problems for the builder as the home is erected. A good foundation is just that. The boards can also be raised or lowered to make the strings marking the foundation level.

You can check the square of your strings by measuring diagonally across rectangular foundations or by using a little high school math. Measure along one string six feet out from the corner and mark it with chalk. Measure out eight feet on the other corner string and mark it. The distance between the six and eight foot marks should be ten feet.

The purpose of the footing is to transfer the building loads (wall, floor, roof) into the soil. The width and depth of the footing varies with the size and weight of the home as well as the type of soil. If the soil has a tendency to shift, freeze, or compact, piers (columns of concrete) are poured below the footing for vertical support.

To begin the footing, first dig a trench wider than the proposed footing and to approximately the footing's base. (In colder climates, the footing should be below the frost line.) Then drop a plumb bob from your batter board strings to the footing grade. This marks the outside edge of your foundation wall. Measure out to the edges of the footing and mark it with a squeeze bottle filled with chalk. To mark the exact horizontal level of your proposed footing, measure down from the string to the top of the eventual footing and drive a stake into the ground so that the top of the stake marks the top of the footing. Repeat this process around the footing trench.

Footing forms can now be built to hold the poured concrete in place until it dries. They are usually made out of wood, though some builders simplify the step by trenching undisturbed soil the required width and depth to serve as natural forms. Forms can be built from lumber that will eventually be used in an unseen portion of the home such as roof framing. Other builders rent concrete forms by the foot.

Reinforcing is important, especially in large homes. The most common method is with A-615 reinforcing bar (called *rebar*) laid in the footing trench and elevated with short vertical sections of rebar stuck in the ground. Some footings also include short sections of rebar bent into L's and set with one angle sticking out of the top of the finished footing. The foundation wall is then attached. This prevents side-slip of the wall.

In most areas, 3000 pound concrete is used for footings and foundations. That is, the concrete has a compressive strength of 3000 pounds per square inch within 28 days of pouring. A transit-mix company can supply 3000 pound concrete or you can mix Portland Cement ASTM C-150, type I or II with 6½ gallons of water per sack. Figure 5½ sacks per cubic yard of concrete. Rock should be uniform ¾ inch grade crushed rock, clean and free of organic material.

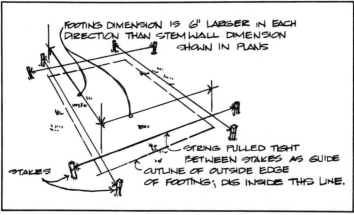

Fig. 7-2. Laying out the foundation (courtesy Beaver Log Homes).

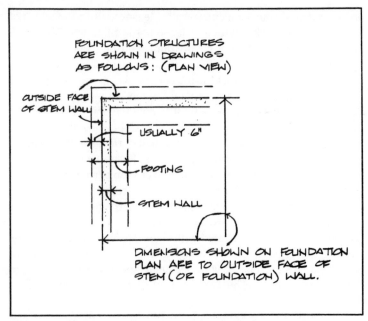

FOUNDATION STRUCTURES ARE SHOWN IN DRAWINGS AS FOLLOWS: (PLAN VIEW)

OUTSIDE FACE OF STEM WALL

USUALLY 6"

FOOTING

STEM WALL

DIMENSIONS SHOWN ON FOUNDATION PLAN ARE TO OUTSIDE FACE OF STEM (OR FOUNDATION) WALL.

Fig. 7-3. Foundation structures are shown in plan drawings as above (courtesy Beaver Log Homes).

In areas where curing time must be shortened or where freeze-thaw action is a problem, you may want to use a concrete additive. Talk with your contractor or cement supplier.

Make sure you have your concrete and reinforcements ready before you begin pouring. Have enough on hand to finish the job. Once the pouring for footing begins, it should continue uninterrupted until it is completed.

Once the concrete is poured into forms it should be tamped or vibrated to make sure the mix surrounds the rebar and hasn't formed air pockets that will weaken the structure. To cure the footings, keep the concrete and forms moist for five to seven days after pouring. Then remove the forms and let them dry out some more before building the forms for your foundation walls.

INSTALLING FOUNDATION WALLS

The foundation wall actually has many names, depending on its height and use. If it's two feet or shorter it's called a *stem wall*. If taller, it's a *foundation wall*. If it encloses below-grade liveable space it's called a *basement wall*. For simplicity, we'll call it a " foundation wall."

There are basically three types of common foundation walls used under modern buildings: poured concrete, concrete block, and stone. All are used to support log homes.

Poured concrete foundations, like poured footings, need forms to contain them until they solidify. Again, the forms can be built with reusable lumber (½- and ¾-inch exterior grade plywood and 2×4s) or rented locally. The forms are built not only to contain the concrete while it's drying, but also to keep the desired shape. Support must be built into the forms so that the mass of concrete doesn't bow the form and make bulges in the foundation wall.

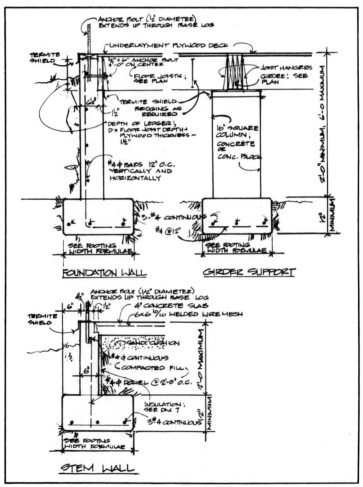

Fig. 7-4. Basic foundation walls (courtesy Beaver Log Homes).

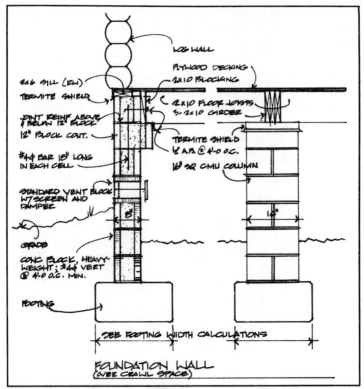

Fig. 7-5. Foundation wall over crawl space (courtesy Beaver Log Homes).

Concrete foundation walls cure best when poured on cool days—between 40 and 80 degrees—when humidity is moderate or high. The concrete should not dry out too fast or it will not be as strong and bonded. As with the footings, keep it wet for the first week.

Once the forms are taken down, you should moisture-proof the concrete with either asphalt cement applied with a brush or cement mortar.

To start a concrete block foundation wall, spread a mortar bed on the footing at one corner of your building. Then lay the corner blocks and tamp them down into place with the handle of the trowel. Check for level. Do a few more, laying mortar below and between each block about ⅜ inches thick. Run a mason's line to the next corner to make sure the blocks are being laid straight and level.

To reinforce a concrete block wall you can either lay a wire mesh within the mortar in every third course or pour concrete and place rebar into some of the hollows in the blocks once you're done. Local building codes may dictate the type and method of reinforcement.

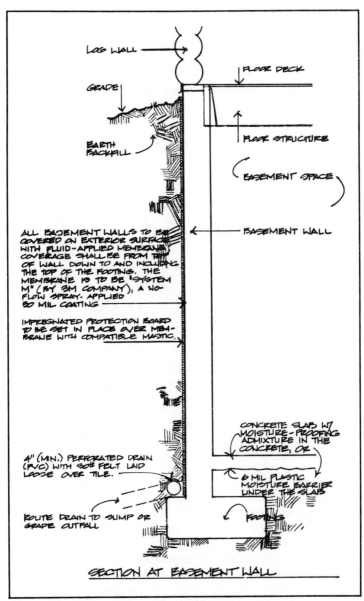

Fig. 7-6. Basement wall foundation (courtesy Beaver Log Homes).

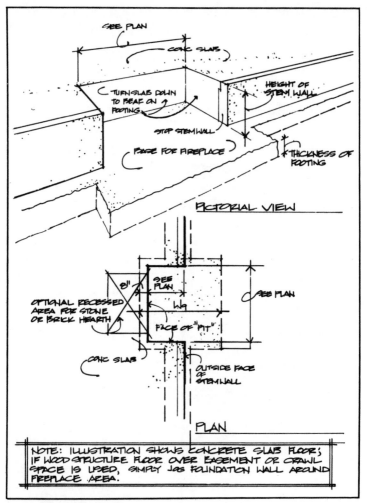

Fig. 7-7. Fireplace slab (courtesy Beaver Log Homes).

You can vent the crawl space by replacing one block with a vent as you build. The best rule is one vent for every 300 feet of floor space—four to six for the average home. They are usually installed four feet from the corners and eight inches above ground level, about four inches into the wall.

Working with stones is trickier. Many builders prefer to have experienced stone foundation subcontractors install the foundation. The stone foundation requires a thickness of 18 to 24 inches so your footing should be wider than normal to support the weight of the stones. Key factors in building a stone wall or foundation are integration and bonding. The stones need to be carefully chosen to match the size and shape of neighboring stones. Bonding is done by laying a bond stone every three or four courses to hold the wall together. (A bond stone is one that is as thick as the wall.) The top course should be of larger bond stones with the flat surface up.

An alternative is to hand-lay small stones in the concrete as it is being poured into forms. Stones are laid flat-side-out toward the exterior of the foundation from ground level to the top.

Another method of building a foundation under your log home is with piers. As mentioned earlier, piers are simply columns of concrete. The simplest method is to dig a two foot hole with a post hole digger every six to twelve feet along major flooring timbers and pour concrete into them so that all are at the same top level. Then set pyramid piers on top of each footing. You can also use cylindrical fiber forms that look like a large tube. You dig a round hole, install the form and pack dirt around it, make sure it's in position, and pour concrete into the form. Once it's dry, you simply peel away the fiber form and your piers are ready to use.

Less commonly used is the slab foundation. It's made by building a shallow form to contain the poured concrete, laying rebar as needed, lining the bottom with gravel, and pouring a level cement floor. A vapor barrier should be laid before the foundation is poured.

Problems with slab floors include high energy loss and a tendency to crack and shift with the earth below. They are used primarily in areas where the foundation must be built quickly and where soils are too soft for standard footings and foundation walls.

The top of your foundation wall is tied into your first course of logs with anchor bolts or straps. Bolts can be placed in the wet cement about four feet apart as it sets up in the form. Concrete block walls are capped with mortar, which can hold anchor bolts for the sill plate. Concrete piers are both reinforced and prepared for attachment to wood with long anchor bolts or straps.

SOLVING FOUNDATION PROBLEMS

If you're including a fireplace in your log home you will need a foundation for it. Most builders simply expand their footing into a small slab under the place where the fireplace will be built. They also modify the form of the foundation wall to allow for the structure depending on the size and material.

Any foundation wall over 48 inches high needs additional reinforcement, especially if there will be backfill against it. Here's where you need an expert. If you don't want to hire a professional to install larger foundation walls, you can sometimes hire an assistant who has concrete experience. However, the foundation of your home is the last place you want to skimp on quality.

Hillsides present another problem to building: shifting earth. Larger footings are needed to reduce the chance of movement and stress. Footings are often poured in an L shape to reduce slippage. Again, it's best if an expert at least designs them for you.

If cracks appear in your foundation once it's cured, check for the cause. It may simply be the contraction of the cement due to loss of water. However, it may also point to a bigger problem, such as inadequate footing, inadequate reinforcement, poor cement, poor curing, or unconsidered stress. Call an expert in to pinpoint the problem and come up with a quick solution. It may be costly, but the longer the problem lives, the greater the cost.

A good foundation is the best place to start a good log home.

Chapter 8

Building Floors and Decks

Laying the floor for your log home begins with a close check of your foundation. You'll want to know:

- [ ] Overall dimensions of the foundation wall.
- [ ] Location of pier columns and footings.
- [ ] Anchor rod location and spacing.

Also, make sure that your foundation is cured. It should be at least two weeks and preferably a month old if made of poured concrete or stone. Concrete block foundations can be a little younger.

The *sill* joins the walls to the foundation. There are two types of sills commonly used in log home construction: *log sill* and *box sill*. Log sill is preferred by traditionalists while box sill construction is adapted from frame houses and is suggested by many log home kit manufacturers. Consider both and choose the one that best fits your home.

INSTALLING LOG SILLS

The longest and best logs should be chosen as sill logs. Splices should be kept to a minimum, and preferably over anchor rods or bolts. You can either mill one side of the log flat or begin the wall with a half log base. Install a metal termite shield between the foundation and the sill log.

Before the sill log can be set in place, transfer the bolt locations from the foundation to the log and drill holes so that the bolts can be

Fig. 8-1. Completed foundation ready for 2×10 sill plate to be installed (courtesy New England Log Homes, Inc.).

run through the log. Countersink the holes so that the bolts don't extend up into the second course of logs. Lay a seal down before installing the log, place the log, and then tighten it down into position.

Log sills are joined at the corner by a number of methods, depending on the corner joints planned for your home. The most practical is the mortise and tenon joint. A *mortise* or notch is made in the first sill log and a *tenon* that will fit into the mortise is cut at the end of the second sill log. They are fit together and sealed. The second sill log is anchored and the first course—the *sill course*—is in place.

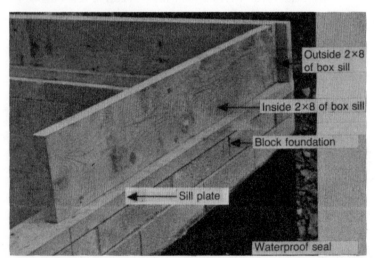

Fig. 8-2. Cement block foundation with sill plate in place and partial box sill construction (courtesy Northern Products Log Homes, Inc.).

You can also notch the sill log corners with a standard saddle joint. Lay the second sill log across the first log, mark the notch, cut it out, and fit the corner together. The saddle joint and other notches will be explained further in Chapter 10 as you build your log walls.

Once the sills are in place, the joists must be installed. The floor joists form a level frame over which the subfloor is laid. There are a number of popular ways of attaching the floor joists to the sill

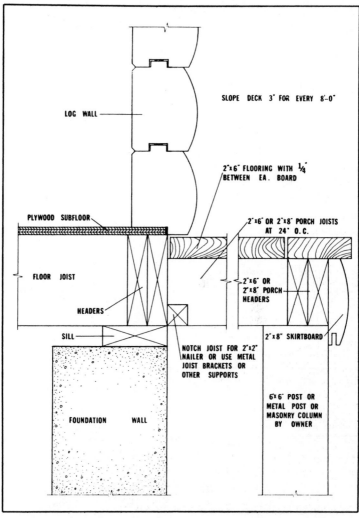

Fig. 8-3. View of foundation with box sill and subfloor including details of porch addition.

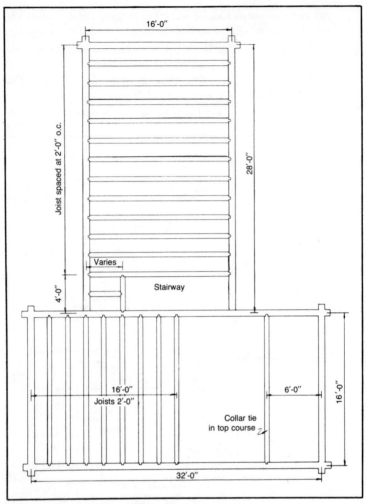

Fig. 8-4. Joist plan (courtesy New England Log Homes, Inc.).

and foundation. One is the mortise and tenon technique just used in joining sill log corners. The sill logs are notched and the joist log ends are cut to fit the mortise, then nailed in place. The joists are also notched on the bottom to fit over the girder that runs the length of the foundation for support.

Another method of installing joists is to build the foundation with a sill on the inside that will support the ends of joists so that their tops are level with the top of the foundation. This method can be used with either log or dimensional lumber joists.

Fig. 8-5. Installing 2 × 10 floor joists on 16-inch centers using steel joist hangers at non-pocket loadbearing beam (courtesy New England Log Homes, Inc.).

Still another method is to mill the inside edge of the sill logs flat and nail "hangers" into place that will support the ends of your joists. This is a modification of the way joists are installed in box sill construction.

INSTALLING BOX SILLS

Box sill construction simplifies the process by building a box that sits between the foundation and the log walls. It contains all the components: sill, joists, and bracing. It's simple and complete.

Fig. 8-6. Cantilever construction (courtesy Pan Abode Cedar Homes).

Fig. 8-7. The completed joist system (courtesy Pan Abode Cedar Homes).

Most box sills are made with 2×10 dimensional lumber, though smaller homes only need 2×8 box sills. The first step is installing the sill plate, a dimensional board as wide as the foundation wall (8, 10 or 12 inches) and two inches thick. Tighten it into place with the anchor bolts, countersunk slightly.

Next, a 2×10 is stood at the outside edge of the sill plate parallel to the girder and toe-nailed into place. This board is called the *header joist* or *ribbon*. The "stringer" joist is stood on the joining sill and the two are nailed together. This is done all around the foundation.

Then the floor joists are installed. They are also of 2×10 lumber, running between the stringer joist and the girder spaced 16 inches apart. The easiest installation of floor joists is with hangers nailed to the stringer and girder.

Fig. 8-8. Installing subflooring over the joists (courtesy Pan Abode Cedar Homes).

116

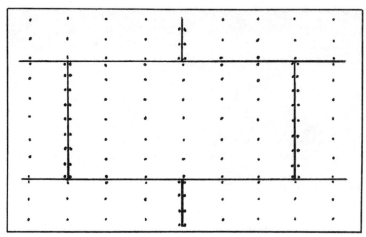

Fig. 8-9. Plywood subfloor nailing pattern (courtesy Pan Abode Cedar Homes).

If you prefer the look of logs, you can set the header and stringer joists in a few inches and nail a quarter log face to the outside of the box sill. No one will ever know.

If you're building your log home on piers, the sill will have to be stronger. No problem if you are using logs for your sills, but a box sill should be built with two or even three thicknesses of 2×10s for support.

Bracing between joists is made with either solid blocking or cross-bridging. Solid blocking is simply installing short 2×10 chunks of lumber between the joists and nailing them into place. Cross-bridging uses 2×4s from the top of one joist to the bottom of the next in the form of an X. Special bridging is often needed around the perimeter of your log home to support the tremendous weight of the logs.

Fig. 8-10. Finished subfloor (courtesy Pan Abode Cedar Homes).

Fig. 8-11. Foundation is backfilled (courtesy New England Log Homes, Inc.).

INSTALLING SUBFLOORING

The subflooring of any home (log or frame) is the plywood nailed over the top of the joists that becomes the base for interior floors. Most subfloor is ⅝ inch CDX grade plywood, either tongue and groove or plain. It comes in 4×8 foot sheets.

Begin at the corner of the house where you began the joist layout. To ensure proper alignment of the first row, strike a chalk line across the joists 4 feet ⅛ inch in from the outside edge of the stringer. Lay the first sheet and tack it down with a few 8d (eight penny) galvanized box nails. Continue laying sheets across the joists in a row until you reach the other end. Trim off the end parallel with the outside of your box sill.

Start the next row of subflooring with a half sheet (4×4 feet) so that they are staggered. The third row begins with a full sheet. Odd shapes can be filled in with scrap.

Once the subfloor has been nailed and trimmed, install the wood drip cap using 8d nails.

You're done! If your subfloor will be sitting for a while before wall construction begins, cover the deck with four mil black plastic.

SOLVING FLOOR AND DECK PROBLEMS

You may need to cut holes in the subfloor for fireplaces, a stairway, trap door, or chimney. The outline of the hole should be marked on the subfloor as it is laid over it. If the hole is smaller than the gap between joists, you can frame the hole with smaller dimensional lumber. It's easier if you do it before you lay the subflooring.

Insulation can be installed over the floor joists before the subfloor is laid and nailed down. Or it can be tucked in place from underneath after the subfloor is in place. Or it can be sprayed on from below if there is room to maneuver. Logs with lower R-factors will require that additional insulation be placed in the floor and ceiling of your home. Check local codes.

Moisture is an enemy of wood. Dry rot can form in woods with more than a 30 percent moisture factor. One way of minimizing moisture in your log home is by laying a sealed sheet of six mil plastic on the ground under your home. It will also help the efficiency of floor insulation.

Decks can be added to your foundation by simply building a frame over concrete piers and attaching it to the box sill or base log with lag bolts. Later, after you've built your log walls and installed the roof, you can add a roof to the deck and turn it into a porch, or enclose it to make a greenhouse.

Chapter 9

Preparing for Log Construction

The logs are on their way. The truck from the mill or kit factory will be here tomorrow morning and you'd better be ready.

A planned delivery can make construction easier, while an unplanned one can add weeks to your schedule. The ideal case is that the truck will easily find your site, back into position and be offloaded within an hour after placing every bundle in the best position for construction. The worst that can happen is that the truck can't get to your site and everything must be offloaded *by hand* a half mile away and hauled to the site in pieces, the resorted. You frantically sign and pay for the load, then find out there are pieces missing.

The difference is simply planning. A couple hours of brain work can save dozens of hours of back work—and many dollars.

TIMING THE DELIVERY

If you're working with a nearby supplier you can often give him a day or two notice and have the materials delivered to your site. However, you may end up ordering a shell or even a complete kit from a distant factory. If so, give them these instructions: Call you as soon as the truck leaves the factory, have the driver call about 24 hours before he expects to arrive (for final directions to the site), and make sure the delivery is made in the morning so everything is done before it gets dark.

When the factory, mill, or supplier calls, you can ask for an

Fig. 9-1. A final call to the factory and the truck is loaded and on its way (courtesy Northeastern Log Homes, Inc.).

estimate of transit time, the expected delivery date, the manpower you will need to offload, special equipment needed, and how much money you must have for the driver, including any C.O.D. charges. Then begin planning out the delivery. Contact your crew—you'll need four to eight healthy workers to unload the truck depending on what equipment you (or the truck) have. Get a few back-up workers in case some of the crew doesn't show up.

Don't plan on doing any of the offloading yourself. Instead, act as supervisor, checking components as they come off the truck and showing workers where to place them. Make sure you have *everything* before you sign for it. If you are working with a kit dealer or factory representative he can help you in the checking and sorting of materials, but you still should be there supervising—it's *your* house.

If your logs come from a mill they will probably be delivered on a standard log truck. A kit from a factory will be on a flatbed truck. Materials from a builders' supply will either be on a small flatbed or box bed truck. In any case, you must make sure that the truck can get to your site. Check it for road condition, obstacles and turn-around.

The road to your site must be able to carry up to 80,000 pounds,

Fig. 9-2. Some kits are delivered on boom trailers with hoists to unload the kit at your site (courtesy New England Log Homes, Inc.).

Fig. 9-3. Boom trailer hoist in action (courtesy New England Log Homes, Inc.).

depending on the truck used. Many builders prefer winter deliveries in cold climates so the roads won't be soft. Spring in a wet area can make roads impassable to heavy trucks. If in doubt, talk with an experienced trucker. Also make sure that there are no obstacles that would hamper delivery such as small bridges or steep grades. Make sure that the truck has room to maneuver and turn around at your site. Don't expect him to back all the way out. The alternative is to have the driver come as far as he can safely, and your crew offloads there. If there's an experienced truck driver in

Fig. 9-4. Some kits are delivered on standard boom cab trucks (courtesy Pan Abode Cedar Homes).

your crew have him meet the truck somewhere and guide him to the site.

Your logs or kit may be delivered by railroad car. If so, the freight office will call you when the car is in at a nearby siding and will tell you when it must be completely unloaded—usually within 48 hours. A crew and flatbed truck will take six to eight hours, depending on the size of the load and the docking available.

Fig. 9-5. You can also offload your kit with a fork lift (courtesy New England Log Homes, Inc.).

Fig. 9-6. You can offload materials by hand (courtesy Northern Products Log Homes, Inc.).

UNLOADING YOUR MATERIAL

You may have ordered a boom trailer for delivery of your logs. If so, the driver will lift the packages off the back of the trailer and set them nearby. With luck, he's been able to position the truck close enough to the building site to minimize handling. If not, you'll have to break the packages and resort later.

You can also rent or hire an all-terrain forklift to unload your materials. In this case, make sure you coordinate delivery times with the operator to minimize the cost. Make sure he knows where everything is to be placed.

If unloading equipment is too costly or unavailable, you may have to offload the materials by hand. To minimize handling, have areas marked out for each type of material so that your crew can place it quickly and easily.

Dunnage (such as 4×4s) should be placed where you want materials stacked. This will prevent the logs and components from becoming soiled and damaged. If the logs won't be used for awhile, lay 1×1 slats between rows of logs so that air can circulate around them.

Doors and windows should be handled carefully, stacked, and covered to protect them from the weather. It's best to build a small weather-tight shack for tools, doors, and windows on your site. Subflooring should also be covered.

SIGNING FOR DELIVERY

Once everything is off the truck you can sign for the delivery and pay the driver or dealer. Note any obvious damage to the materials right on the Bill of Lading the driver supplies. If it is severe, call the trucking claim office. Factories won't ship broken or

Fig. 9-7. Many hands make light work (courtesy Lincoln Logs Ltd.,).

Fig. 9-8. Trusses come off first (courtesy Lincoln Logs Ltd.,).

damaged materials and the trucking firm won't accept them, so you can rightfully assume that damage was done in transit.

When you sign the Bill of Lading and other paperwork, note "Materials received, but not inventoried." You cannot hold up the driver while you check to make sure that every piece is there, but you should inventory it the same day, before materials are sorted and stored. In some cases, the driver is willing to "take lunch" while you inventory your load carefully and check it against the Bill of Materials from the factory or mill.

Then it's time to pay. You will probably be asked to have a certified check for the balance made out to the factory, mill, or supplier on hand. You give it to either the driver or the factory representative, as directed. You may also be required to pay the driver for transportation. Most will accept a personal check from you.

SORTING AND STORING

Some kits come bundled into walls so that pre-sorting is almost unnecessary. If these bundles are placed near the working area, you may only have to open them up and start building.

However, most kits and all scratch logs should be sorted once they are delivered and before construction begins. Logs you've cut and prepared yourself or had milled locally can be sorted and stacked by type and use—sill logs, short logs, purloins, posts, and full wall logs.

Kit logs are often marked on the top surface for size and location. As an example, Pan Abode may mark a log—actually a milled timber—"LL 16 C-YY" meaning it is the 16th timber in the LL wall that runs from the C to the YY wall. You'll stack it with other LL wall timbers near the C and YY wall piles.

Some logs and timbers may have special designations such as "Riptung," meaning the top timber in a full timber exterior wall, or "WDO" for a window timber.

Each manufacturer will have his own marking codes and code-breaking system. Many will even have specific instructions on how to best sort logs for easiest wall building. You can perform your inventory while logs are sorted to ensure that everything is at the

Fig. 9-9. If you have a large enough crew, carry logs directly to the building site (courtesy Lincoln Logs, Ltd.).

Fig. 9-10. Sort and stack logs by their eventual location (courtesy Northeastern Log Homes).

site. If not, contact your dealer or the factory about getting missing parts before you begin construction.

If construction won't begin for a few weeks, cover your materials well, especially doors and windows that can be damaged by the elements. Logs can also be covered with plastic sheeting, anchor the plastic on the sides as you would a tent to allow air to circulate under the cover and dry out the logs. Most are cut and milled green.

Sometimes overlooked are the so-called little things. As you inventory and sort your materials make sure you have adequate caulking, splines, spikes, butyl rope, insulation strips, sealer foam, nails, doors, windows, frames, and other parts. A shortage of spikes can hold up construction just as well as a shortage of logs.

Your blueprints should be handy during the delivery and sorting of materials, logs, and kits in case there are questions of placement, size, or number of components. Some builders make a portable easel with a clear plastic cover to protect the prints from the elements while still making them visible. The easel can be stored in your tool shed or carried in the back of your car. It's best to have it on-site for building inspectors, contractors, and subcontractors.

GETTING HELP

Again, if you're buying a kit from a dealer within a hundred miles of your building site you'll probably have a number of helpful visits from him as you plan and build your log home. Some may even want to take pictures of your progress for other customers.

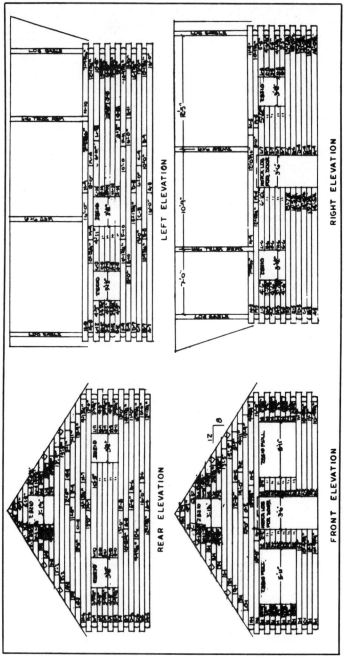

Fig. 9-11. Check your elevation diagram for placement of logs (courtesy Northern Products Log Homes, Inc.).

129

If you buy directly from the factory you can get a telephone number for problems—usually a sales manager or engineer who can explain solutions over the phone or plan to visit the site if necessary.

If you're building on your own from site-cut logs you can line up expert help in advance through log home building schools or experienced log builders. For an hourly rate they can be called to answer questions on construction or travel for on-site assistance. Even if you have log home construction experience, it's best to have someone whom you can call when seemingly unsolvable problems arise.

Help is also available through factory-written construction guides, books such as this and S. Blackwell Duncan's *How To Build Your Own Log Home & Cabin From Scratch* (TAB Book No. 1081), and publications such as *Log Home Guide*. The more facts you have on hand and available, the easier it will be to prepare for construction of your own log home.

Chapter 10

Building Log Walls

The fun begins. Until now you've just been preparing: planning your home, selecting your building site, gathering materials, cutting logs, or ordering kits and laying the foundation. Now you can begin to see some progress as the log walls are erected. With just a few days of work your log home will take shape.

Don't be nervous. Thousands of log homes have been built and thousands more will be. And each is constructed with the same three elements: materials, knowledge, and planning. You have all three available.

ERECTING ROUGH LOG WALLS

We're calling any log that's been prepared by the owner a "scratch" or "rough" log. You may have cut and cured your own logs right on the building site or you may have had them cut for you and delivered so you could debark and treat them. In any case, they are not fully milled, jointed, and notched. You'll do some of this as you build your home from rough logs.

While some log homes are still being built with fully rounded logs, most are being modified with an axe or chain saw to fit together tighter and reduce "chinking" or sealing between the logs. This joint can be made in many ways.

Flat joints are cut with a chain saw, axe or, one-man lumber mill by ripping two opposing sides flat so that the log can stack easily. Set the log across dunnage logs and lock it into place with log dogs,

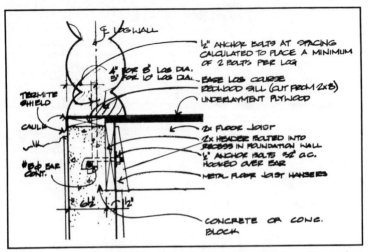

Fig. 10-1. Half log base floor structure at perimeter (courtesy Beaver Log Homes).

nail a guide board to the side of the log, and rip. You'll have an even cut. If you want to further reduce chinking and sealing, simply run your chain saw along the log, cutting a groove on the top and bottom so that a *spline* board can be inserted as the logs are stacked.

Round joints are made by setting and locking your log on dunnage boards, then hewing out a concave groove along one side of the log with a gutter adze. This groove will fit over the round top of the lower log as you build.

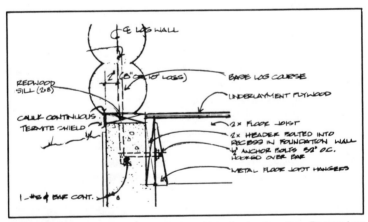

Fig. 10-2. Whole log base floor structure at perimeter (courtesy Beaver Log Homes).

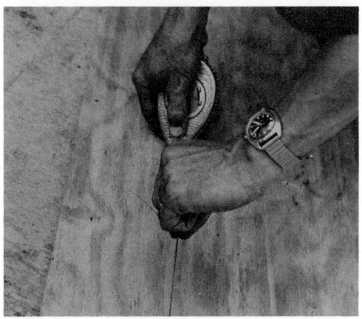

Fig. 10-3. Snap a chalk line to mark the first log course (courtesy Lincoln Logs, Ltd.).

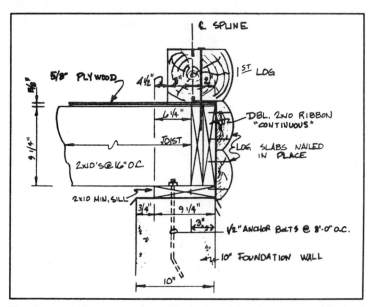

Fig. 10-4. Attaching the base course log to the subfloor (courtesy New England Log Homes, Inc.).

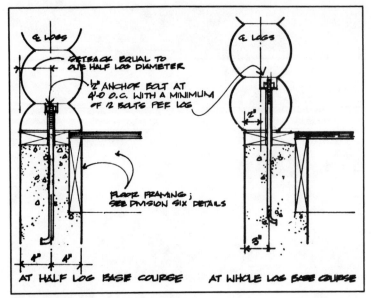

Fig. 10-5. Base log course attachment (courtesy Beaver Log Homes).

V joints are cut with a chain saw by placing the log on dunnage logs, setting another against it, and locking them both into place with log dogs. Then a chain saw is run between them to make a flat cut. Next, the logs are rolled about 60 degrees (one-sixth of the circumference) and cut again in the same way. The female groove is

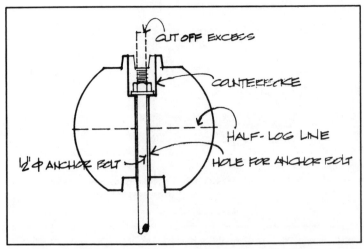

Fig. 10-6. Installing an anchor bolt (courtesy Beaver Log Homes).

134

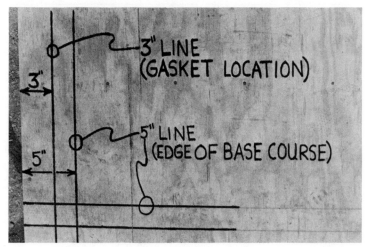

Fig. 10-7. Log and gasket locations (courtesy New England Log Homes, Inc.).

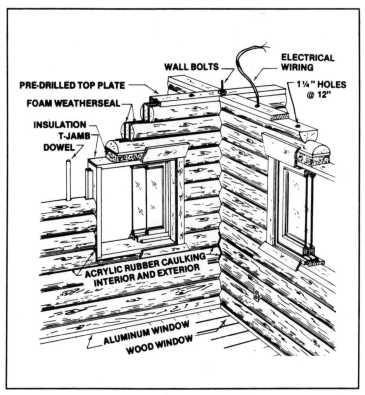

Fig. 10-8. Basic log wall construction (courtesy Lok-Log, Inc.).

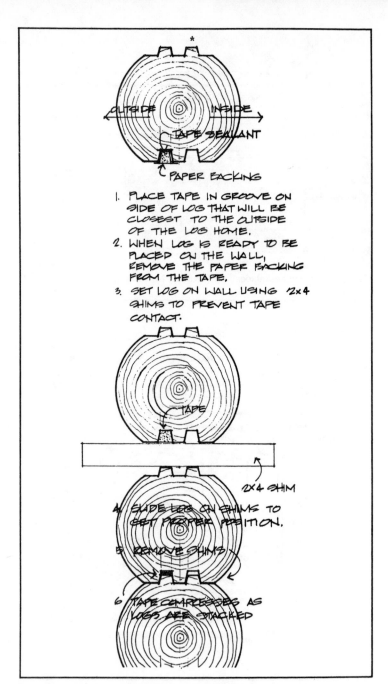

Fig. 10-9. Installing tape sealant (courtesy Beaver Log Homes).

made with a circular saw guided by a board nailed to the bottom of the log.

The major difficulty with stacking rough logs is their varied sizes and shapes. This can be overcome somewhat by jointing and stacking them relative to the center of each log. That is, draw a straight line through the heart of the log on the ends before jointing.

Another problem is getting them up on the wall, as rough logs are often cut larger than kit logs. This can be done either with a block and tackle, an electric winch, or by using ramp logs placed from the wall to the ground and used to roll the logs up into position by hand.

Once into place you can notch them to fit together on the corners with this four step method:

1. *Scribe the notch.* Using log dogs to secure your log, measure the gap between the log and the one below it with a scribe tool. Now outline the curvature of the lower log onto the upper log, scribing or scratching the outline onto the top log.

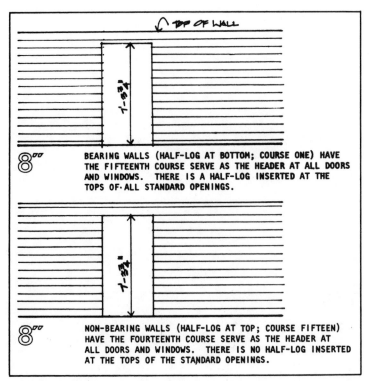

BEARING WALLS (HALF-LOG AT BOTTOM; COURSE ONE) HAVE THE FIFTEENTH COURSE SERVE AS THE HEADER AT ALL DOORS AND WINDOWS. THERE IS A HALF-LOG INSERTED AT THE TOPS OF·ALL STANDARD OPENINGS.

NON-BEARING WALLS (HALF-LOG AT TOP; COURSE FIFTEEN) HAVE THE FOURTEENTH COURSE SERVE AS THE HEADER AT ALL DOORS AND WINDOWS. THERE IS NO HALF-LOG INSERTED AT THE TOPS OF THE STANDARD OPENINGS.

Fig. 10-10. Figuring log courses (courtesy Beaver Log Homes).

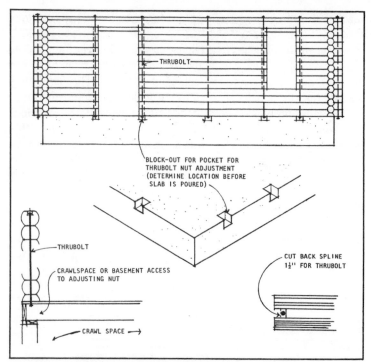

Fig. 10-11. Log wall thrubolting (courtesy Beaver Log Homes).

Fig. 10-12. Attaching aluminum flashing to bottom of base log using Masonite spline to flashing into groove until it's bent and stapled to the log (courtesy New England Log Homes, Inc.).

Fig. 10-13. Align the spline groove by using a mason's line or chalk line (courtesy New England Log Homes, Inc.).

2. *Cut the notch.* Loosen the log dog and roll the log back so that the scribe is up. Now slice into the notch with a chain saw or axe. Then clean out the notch with a draw knife or wood chisel and mallet.

3. *Check the notch.* Roll the log back into position and make sure the notch fits the log below it tightly and that the logs fit snugly all along their edges.

Fig. 10-14. Door jamb is plumbed and braced (courtesy New England Log Homes, Inc.).

Fig. 10-15. Spike hole is drilled in first course (courtesy New England Log Homes, Inc.).

4. *Seal the log.* Finally, separate the logs one last time to place your spline, insulation and sealer between the logs. Refit them, then spike the logs together in countersunk holes.

Windows and doors can be cut out of solid log walls by making notches in the top of the highest log to be cut so that you can get your chain saw started once you're ready to cut the openings. Nail guide boards to the inside of the wall where doors and windows will be cut. Make sure they are level to ensure a square opening.

There are many ways you can install utilities in a home built of solid rough logs. The simplest is to have all outlets, switches, and piping within interior stud walls. If this isn't always practical, you can also build your base course with a false-faced log. That is, you

Fig. 10-16. First course of logs is spiked into place on 2½ foot centers (courtesy New England Log Homes, Inc.).

Fig. 10-17. Spiking corner joints (courtesy New England Log Homes, Inc.).

Fig. 10-18. Turning a corner with a stack section (courtesy New England Log Homes, Inc.).

141

Fig. 10-19. End two stack sections at a corner to prevent dead-ending into jambs (courtesy New England Log Homes, Inc.).

trim off the face of the log, cut or build a groove into the new face, run your wires or pipes, then replace the old face and bring services out through it as necessary. You can also run some wiring up through door casings to switches located next to doors.

Fig. 10-20. Before laying logs, staple tar paper along the sill plate or deck edge (courtesy Lincoln Logs Ltd.).

Rounded rough logs can be sealed from the interior and exterior of the home by a process called *chinking*. A chink is a crack in a wall, and chinking is done with mortar or plaster. Better still is plastic cement that will not dry out and crumble as quickly, but it's best to cut and fit logs so that chinking is unnecessary.

BUILDING WALLS WITH KIT LOGS

Logs supplied in log home kits are much easier to work with for many reasons. First, they are already jointed to fit snugly together. Second, they are saddle notched by machine to ensure a tight fit at corners. Third, they are uniform in size and approximate length to

Fig. 10-21. Spiking the first log into place (courtesy Lincoln Logs Ltd.).

Fig. 10-22. Spikes near a joint should be carefully set (courtesy Lincoln Logs Ltd.).

make handling and stacking easier. And, fourth, they already have door and window openings planned and cut. There is less waste.

There are disadvantages, too. One is that they cost more than cutting your own. A simple shell kit will cost about $10 a square foot of floor space or about $60 per linear foot of wall. Another disadvantage is that when the logs are made uniform, much of the personality of individual logs is removed. Of course, they still have more "personality" than dimensional lumber. It's a trade-off.

If you've purchased a log home kit you also probably got a

construction guide or instructions, on how to stack and seal the logs together. Just as logs, joints, and notches are unique with each manufacturer, so are the directions, but they still have much in common. We'll discuss the common points and expect you to read and follow your manufacturer's guide as well.

All construction begins with reviewing your blueprints with your crew to make sure that everyone knows how and where logs are placed, spiked, and sealed as well as where doors and windows will be installed.

The base course or first row of logs on your subfloor are often half-logs with the joints facing up. Install these around the entire perimeter of your home wherever you will have a log wall. Some manufacturers even suggest you install the base course through

Fig. 10-23. For a straight notch corner, start by matching the logs (courtesy Lincoln Logs Ltd.).

Fig. 10-24. Mark the corner with a pencil (courtesy Lincoln Logs Ltd.).

where doors will eventually be to ensure alignment, then cut out the log after the wall is built. Mark your subfloor with a snap line before starting and you will have a guide for lining up the base course for a good start.

Next, build what are called *bucks* or frames for the windows and doors; these will plug the opening until the real thing is installed. The buck consists of four perimeter boards and cross boards that brace the frame and keep logs from bowing the frame in. Your plans will tell you on which course to mount the window bucks so that they are placed correctly for later installation.

The first full course to be laid is usually the one starting the

Fig. 10-25. Cut the marked notch (courtesy Lincoln Logs Ltd.).

146

Fig. 10-26. Match the corners up (courtesy Lincoln Logs Ltd.).

walls on the gable ends. Lay the log out, join shorter logs together if necessary with notches and spikes, make sure the corner or saddle notches fit together correctly, then spike or bolt them into position. Be careful not to break the joint notch as you spike. It will make stacking the logs much more difficult. You can place a spike in a tight spot by setting a smaller mallet on the spike's head and hitting both with a larger sledge. Some manufacturers suggest you spike every 30 inches along the wall while others prefer 48 inches with staggered spikes on each course. Others use a bolting system with predrilled bolt holes and countersunk nut holes.

Next, the log is sealed in preparation for the laying of the next course of logs. Sealing is done several ways. Some builders use

Fig. 10-27. For a notch-and-pass corner, cut the wood out of the notch (courtesy Lincoln Logs Ltd.).

Fig. 10-28. Chip away the wood until the notch is clean (courtesy Lincoln Logs Ltd.).

foam gaskets that slip into a milled groove. Others use a spline covered with a strip of fiberglass insulation. Still others use a liquid caulking or other sealant spread along the notch and joint of each log. A few use a combination of sealing methods. Sealing the logs is very important, especially for the first year or two of the log home's life. Since most kit logs are cut, milled, and delivered green (not fully dried) and because the weight of the walls will compact them, the building will have small gaps between logs for awhile. Heat loss can be high through an entire wall of these small cracks. Adequate sealing is necessary, at least until the walls settle.

As you seal joints, put extra sealant at the corners. Most

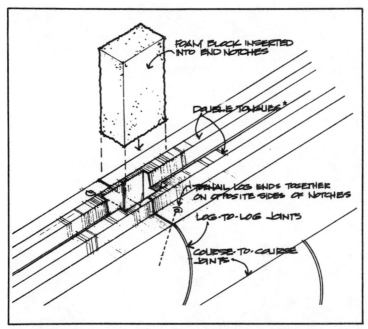

Fig. 10-29. Log-to-log and course-to-course joints (courtesy Beaver Log Homes).

Fig. 10-30. Corners are spiked (courtesy Lincoln Logs Ltd.).

Fig. 10-31. Holes are drilled for log bolts or spikes (courtesy of Lincoln Logs Ltd.).

Fig.10-32. Logs are sealed with foam and caulking (courtesy Lincoln Logs Ltd.).

150

Fig. 10-33. Notch the base course log for later installation of an electrical box (courtesy Lincoln Logs Ltd.).

Fig. 10-34. Continue stacking log walls, sealing and spiking each course as you go (courtesy Lincoln Logs Ltd.).

Fig. 10-35. Stapling PVC gasket to tongue (courtesy Northern Products Log Homes, Inc.).

notches don't have joints in them and air filtration is highest here.

Keep stacking. Some logs will be pre-notched and marked for their exact position in your home while others will be jointed but not notched. You'll have to do this yourself. Also, check each log as you

Fig. 10-36. Run a bead of caulking compound around the outside perimeter of the tongue for a complete weather tight seal (courtesy Northern Products Log Homes, Inc.).

Fig. 10-37. Butt-and-pass corner (courtesy Lincoln Logs Ltd.).

Fig. 10-38. Logs can be lifted onto the wall with a forklift (courtesy Beaver Log Homes).

153

Fig. 10-39. Two men can easily place most manufactured logs (courtesy Beaver Log Homes).

set it into place. Some may need sanding that can't be done once the wall is erected.

Somewhere between the 13th and 16th course (depending on the thickness of your logs), you'll build what's called the "final course." If you started with a half-log, the final course will also be a half-log. Full log walls usually end in full logs. The final course may have to be installed a little differently, depending on the manufacturer and what you plan to do next—start your roof or build a second story. Many final courses have a mortise or notch that will accept

Fig. 10-40. A crew of six can build a log wall home in a weekend (courtesy Beaver Log Homes).

Fig. 10-41. A special wide gasket is laid at corners (courtesy Beaver Log Homes).

log rafters with tenon ends. Others will be flat on the side for the framing of a ceiling. Still others may have a notch on top for a rafter that will make up the base of a cathedral ceiling rafter system. Follow the plans; if you have questions, talk with your dealer or factory rep.

Utilities are installed the same way in kit logs as solid logs with a few exceptions. Some manufacturers hollow out their logs to increase insulation factors (air is the greatest insulator) and to allow for the running of utilities. To run the utilities vertically you simply drill holes down into each course of logs as you place them, but plan ahead. Other manufacturers supply hollow or false-face logs for the

Fig. 10-42. Joints are caulked before installing the next log (courtesy Beaver Log Homes).

Fig. 10-43. The walls go up (courtesy Northeastern Log Homes).

bottom course(s). Others make a special notch in log ends that can be used to splice wall logs together and serve as a utility channel in doorways.

It's suggested that you read your manufacturer's construction guide and the manuals for other log homes not only before you build, but also before you decide which log home to build. Some shell kits need more preparation and skill to build than others.

Fig. 10-44. Nearly finished (courtesy Northeastern Log Homes).

Fig. 10-45. A full notch-and-pass corner (courtesy Lincoln Logs Ltd.).

BUILDING WITH TIMBERS

A few log home kits are actually built with *timbers* rather than true logs. The difference is that a timber is milled on all four sides. It's not quite dimensional lumber, but it's also not a log anymore. A

Fig. 10-46. Interior corner (courtesy Lincoln Logs Ltd.).

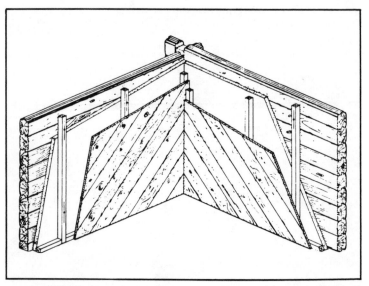

Fig. 10-47. Exterior timber wall and interior insulation and sheathing (courtesy Pan Abode Cedar Homes).

timber home is built by the same stacked wall method. Two of the largest timber home kit manufacturers are Justus and Pan Abode, and both use western red cedar.

The timber is lighter and easier to use than a full log. Splicing

Fig. 10-48. Timbers in place for wall construction (courtesy Pan Abode Cedar Homes).

Fig. 10-49. Milled timber corner (courtesy Pan Abode Cedar Homes).

joints aren't necessary. Interior walls can be made of the same material. They are easier to finish and maintain than log walls. One disadvantage is that the timbers are thinner than full logs and often require double-wall construction to meet insulation codes. Double-wall means greater efficiency—and greater expense.

Fig. 10-50. Spiking the first timber course (courtesy Pan Abode Cedar Homes).

Fig. 10-51. The timber wall goes up quickly (courtesy Pan Abode Cedar Homes).

Double-wall construction does make installing utilities easier. They can be placed between the walls as the walls are erected. Thicker timber walls with single-wall construction must run utilities in interior walls or base courses just like full log homes.

The cost of timber homes is often greater than simpler log homes for many reasons. First, western red cedar is usually more

Fig. 10-52. Starter timbers run through all door openings (courtesy Pan Abode Cedar Homes).

expensive than the pines and spruces used in log construction. Second, more milling is done to the log to make it into a timber and more work means more cost. Also, timber homes often contain more corners, angles, and notches than homes made of larger logs. Third, double-wall construction demanded by smaller timbers means you need more wood. How these factors balance each other is an individual judgement. Some feel they are too "manufactured" while others suggest they are an excellent compromise between log and conventional frame construction.

Chapter 11

Installing Windows and Doors

Your selection and installation of doors and windows can make a great difference in both the beauty and efficiency of your log home. Some log home builders prefer to make their own doors and windows from dimensional boards or facings from milled logs. Doors are not difficult, but windows can present problems as panes and sashes need special tools and skills.

Others prefer the convenience of manufactured doors and windows purchased from local building material firms or with precut log home kits. They are more expensive, but are easier to install and often more efficient—especially double and triple glass windows.

Still others fill the holes in their log walls with secondhand doors and windows purchased through scrap lumber yards and direct from demolition companies. If purchased in advance of construction, they can build around the unique sizes and styles they select. The cost is often half that of new components.

Your choice depends on your building budget, what's available locally, and how handy you are at building your own. For most of us, the cheapest way to go is to buy them pre-built.

WINDOWS

A *sash* is a single frame with one or more *lights* or pieces of glass. Most windows are made of two sashes, one stationary and one movable, either horizontally or vertically. Building a double-sash window requires tools and skill beyond the typical do-it-yourselfer.

Fig. 11-1. Nailing jamb-sill to logs. Note side braces (courtesy New England Log Homes, Inc.).

How you install your windows depends on how you are building your log home. A log wall built with rough logs will usually be constructed without window cuts. Then, when the wall is finished, a chain saw is used to make openings. Some rough log wall builders will make window cuts as the log courses are laid. Still others cut each course to the correct length before stacking and sealing the log. Most kits are precut for window openings.

Fig. 11-2. Window jamb being toe-nailed into logs. Short section of logs stacked next to door (courtesy New England Log Homes, Inc.).

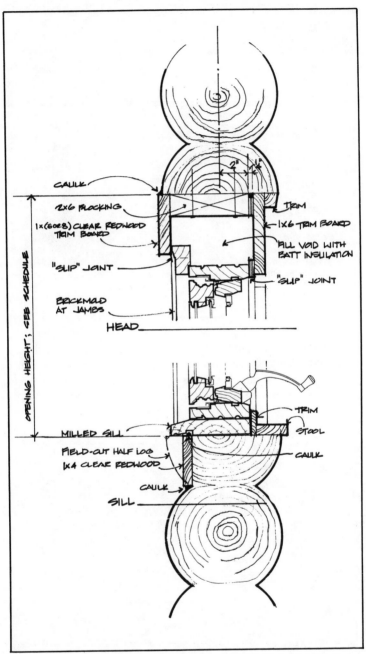

CAULK
2x6 BLOCKING
1x(6 OR 8) CLEAR REDWOOD TRIM BOARD
"SLIP" JOINT
BRICKMOLD AT JAMBS

2"   1"
TRIM
1x6 TRIM BOARD
FILL VOID WITH BATT INSULATION
"SLIP" JOINT

OPENING HEIGHT; SEE SCHEDULE

HEAD

MILLED SILL
FIELD-CUT HALF LOG
1x4 CLEAR REDWOOD
CAULK
SILL

TRIM
STOOL
CAULK

Fig. 11-3. Section at typical window installation — half log (courtesy Beaver Log Homes).

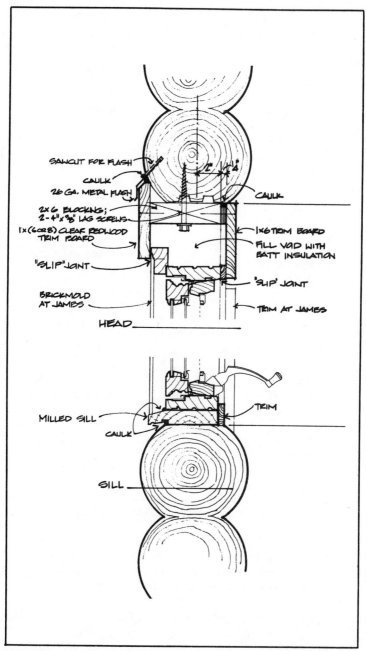

SAWCUT FOR FLASH

CAULK

26 GA. METAL FLASH

2x6 BLOCKNG;
2-4"x⅜" LAG SCREWS

1x(6OR8) CLEAR REDWOOD
TRIM BOARD

"SLIP" JOINT

BRICKMOLD
AT JAMBS

HEAD

CAULK

1x6TRIM BOARD

FILL VOID WITH
BATT INSULATION

'SLIP' JOINT

TRIM AT JAMBS

MILLED SILL

CAULK

TRIM

SILL

Fig. 11-4. Section at typical window installation—whole log (courtesy Beaver Log Homes).

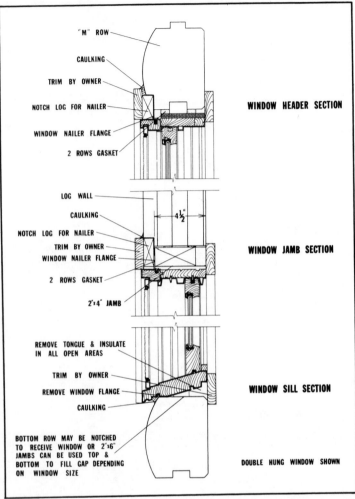

"M" ROW

CAULKING

TRIM BY OWNER

NOTCH LOG FOR NAILER

WINDOW NAILER FLANGE

2 ROWS GASKET

WINDOW HEADER SECTION

LOG WALL

CAULKING

NOTCH LOG FOR NAILER

TRIM BY OWNER

WINDOW NAILER FLANGE

2 ROWS GASKET

2″x4″ JAMB

$4\frac{1}{2}$″

WINDOW JAMB SECTION

REMOVE TONGUE & INSULATE IN ALL OPEN AREAS

TRIM BY OWNER

REMOVE WINDOW FLANGE

CAULKING

BOTTOM ROW MAY BE NOTCHED TO RECEIVE WINDOW OR 2″x6″ JAMBS CAN BE USED TOP & BOTTOM TO FILL GAP DEPENDING ON WINDOW SIZE

WINDOW SILL SECTION

DOUBLE HUNG WINDOW SHOWN

Fig. 11-5. Window installation (courtesy Northern Products Log Homes, Inc.).

Before windows can be installed, the rough openings must be overcut vertically to allow for building settlement. Each log can be expected to shrink ⅛ to ¼ inch, so a gap must be kept at the top of the window opening wide enough to allow for settling of logs around the window.

As an example, a wall of 12 inch rough logs can be expected to have a ¼ inch shrinkage or compaction per log. If your window is three feet (three log courses) tall, you should make the opening at least 36 ¾ inches tall. An opening of 37 inches would be better. This

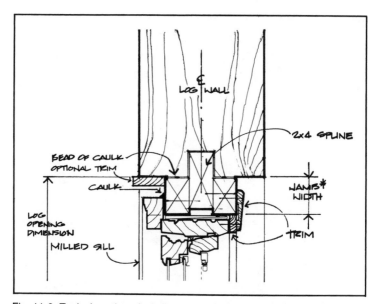

Fig. 11-6. Typical section of window (courtesy Beaver Log Homes).

measurement is to the inside of the frame or buck. You should also nail the frame to the adjoining logs in slotted holes to allow for settling.

The reason for all this is that the shrinkage of the logs as they settle and dry on the wall can put tremendous pressure on the top of windows if there isn't a gap to absorb the impact. The pressure can buckle and shatter frames and windows. So observe this rule of log

Fig. 11-7. Toe-nail the window casing into the log wall (courtesy Pan Abode Cedar Homes).

Fig. 11-8. Installing the door jamb or buck (courtesy New England Log Homes, Inc.).

home building; insulate these gaps well and cover them with molding that will blend into your log home.

Some windows are placed directly into the opening while others require a jamb or casing made of "2 by" dimensional lumber. If you use a jamb, remember to widen your window opening by four inches in each direction to make sure it'll all go together.

Place the window into the opening and make sure everything fits properly. Now check for level and plumb. Most double-sash windows won't operate unless they're completely plumb. Install shims (small pieces of spacing wood) between the window and jambs or logs to align the unit. Once you're satisfied that it's "on the money," nail it in. Some windows are toe-nailed from the logs while others have metal strips that allow them to be nailed into the jamb. Frequently recheck for level and plumb as you install the window. Once it's secure, open and close the window to make sure it'll operate. Then finish it up.

DOORS

Most doors are less complex than windows and can be constructed by the do-it-yourselfer with limited tools and skills. The most popular is the "plank" door made up of vertical planks tied together with horizontal and diagonal bracing—the Z-brace plank door.

Cut lengths of ¾ inch tongue-and-groove stock at least 1½ inches greater than the height of the door frame. Slip them together, sealing each with a weatherproof sealant and holding them in place with pipe clamps. Now lay 2×6 boards horizontally along the top and bottom of the door to the outside edge of the opening. Screw or nail them into place. Then run another 2×6 diagonally from the top

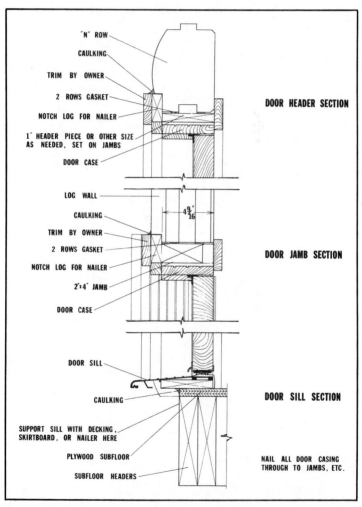

Fig. 11-9. Typical door installation diagram (courtesy Northern Products Log Homes, Inc.).

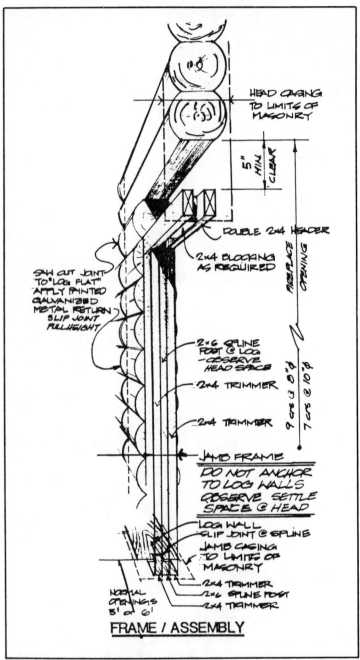

HEAD CASING
TO LIMITS OF
MASONRY

5" MIN CLEAR

DOUBLE 2×4 HEADER

2×4 BLOCKING
AS REQUIRED

SAW CUT JOINT
TO "LOG FLAT"
APPLY PRINTED
GALVANIZED
METAL RETURN
SLIP JOINT
FULL HEIGHT

2×6 SPLINE
POST @ LOG
- OBSERVE
HEAD SPACE

2×4 TRIMMER

2×4 TRIMMER

ROUGH OPENING

9 crs @ 8"∅
7 crs @ 10"∅

JAMB FRAME
DO NOT ANCHOR
TO LOG WALLS
OBSERVE SETTLE
SPACE @ HEAD

LOG WALL
SLIP JOINT @ SPLINE

JAMB CASING
TO LIMITS OF
MASONRY

2×4 TRIMMER
2×6 SPLINE POST
2×4 TRIMMER

NORMAL
OPENINGS
3' or 6'

FRAME / ASSEMBLY

Fig. 11-10. Door frame installation (courtesy Beaver Log Homes).

170

Fig. 11-11. Installing the door jamb (courtesy Northern Products Log Homes, Inc.).

board to the bottom board, cross-bracing the door. Secure it. Attach hinges, an inside handle of wood or metal, a latch, and hang it.

Most exterior doors are 6 foot 8 inches tall and 36 inches wide. Interior doors are the same height and 24 to 32 inches wide depending on needs and available space. Closet doors are smaller than doors to prominent rooms.

Stock doors come in either right or left-hand and are usually prehung—with jambs and hinges. Installing a prehung door is similar to installing a window. Measure the overall door height from the bottom of the sill to the top of the jamb. To this dimension add the maximum settlement allowance (⅛ to ¼ inch per log course). Then

Fig. 11-12. The pre-hung door is installed (courtesy Northern Products Log Homes, Inc.).

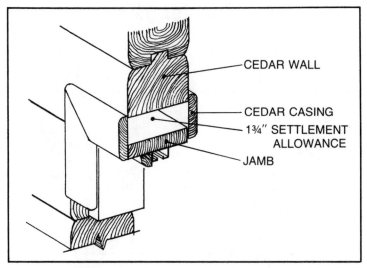

CEDAR WALL

CEDAR CASING
1¾" SETTLEMENT ALLOWANCE

JAMB

Fig. 11-3. The casing covers the door settlement space (courtesy Pan Abode Cedar Homes).

cut the settlement allowance out of the top log or timber using a handsaw or circular saw.

Install the door from the outside of the building. From inside, toe-nail a 16d nail from the log to the back of the door jamb to hold the frame in place. Make sure it's level and plumb, then finish nailing. Stuff the opening around the jamb with fiberglass packing.

Sliding glass doors are installed in a similar manner, making sure that the settlement allowance is adequate to ensure the door won't buckle and break after the log wall settles.

All exterior doors and window casings should be treated immediately to reduce sun bleaching and weather damage.

Chapter 12

Adding a Second Story

A second level or story can be an efficient addition to your log home. It can double the size of your home without doubling construction costs. It's also more efficient to heat and cool than a rambling one-story home of the same size. And it can be easier to live in than a single-story residence.

That's why there's an increasing interest in two-story log homes both from logs and from precut kits. Some builders simply add a few extra log courses to their walls and make it a one-and-a-half story home with loft or attic for extra sleeping and storage. Others make a full second story above with gambrel roof that nearly doubles the size of the original home. A few add a second story to part of the home to reduce the cost-per-square-foot.

But even if you're just planning on topping your single-story home with gable ends, you'll want to read on to learn how it's done.

SECOND FLOOR JOISTS

Once you've reached ceiling height, you can install the ceiling joists which will also serve as second floor joists. The size and span of these joists should be checked by an engineer or architect to make sure they will be adequate to support the additional weight of the second story, as well as maintain lateral strength between side walls. If you're building from a kit, this has probably already been done. Normally, the second floor joists are similar in size, span, and placement to those on the first floor. The major differences are modifications for cathedral ceilings, cuts for stairways, and offset load-bearing walls.

Second-story joist construction begins with the laying of a girder eight to ten inches square through the center of the house. It's supported from the first floor by posts. The girder (or girders) is tied into the outside wall by either a mortise-and-tenon cut or metal brackets, depending on the type and size of girder.

The joists are then placed between the girder and the outside walls by the same method: mortise-and-tenon or metal brackets. It's important that the tops of each girder and joist be milled flat to accommodate the second-story flooring material. Of course, this isn't necessary where the ceiling is open to the roof. Instead, you'll use tie beams.

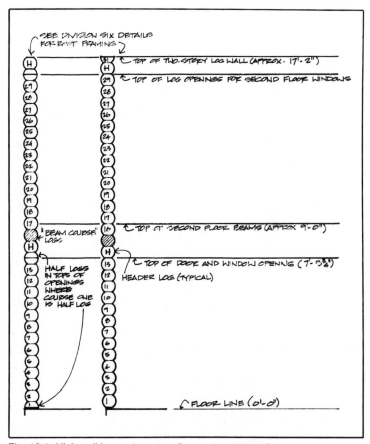

Fig. 12-1. High wall layout (courtesy Beaver Log Homes).

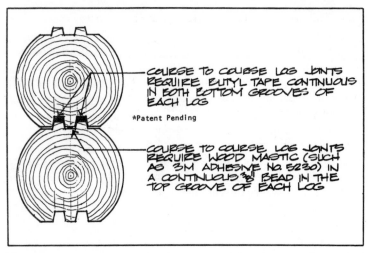

Fig. 12-2. High wall tape and adhesive installation (courtesy Beaver Log Homes).

DECKING

The type of ceiling you install over the first floor level will depend on the material you use to frame it. If all girders, joists, and trusses are of logs you can probably use the bottom of the second-story floor as your ceiling. However, if you've built the framing with dimensional lumber you'll probably cover it with a finish ceiling. The ceiling can then be of plasterboard, paneling, or anything else you want. Most log home builders use conventional framing over rooms where they prefer a conventional ceiling and log framing where they want it exposed.

Dimensional lumber framing is attached to exterior walls much as first floor framing is attached, using a sill and brackets. Log framing is usually tied into outside walls with mortise-and-tenon joints.

Flooring over dimensional frames usually consists of a sub-flooring covered by a finish flooring (carpet, tile, linoleum, wood). It's applied just like the subflooring on the first floor framing. Flooring over a log or timber frame can be the same—subfloor, finish flooring—or it can combine the ceiling, sub and finish into one deck of finish flooring. The most popular is two inch-by-random width tongue-and-groove flooring.

If you're installing finish flooring during this stage of construction, make sure you cover it adequately to prevent weather and workman damage.

WALLS

It's time to add the second-story walls. These walls can range from three to eight feet or more, depending on the roof pitch and usable space desired. A stub or short wall of two to four feet may only give headroom in the center of the second floor—actually a half story, making it a one-and-a-half story home. A knee wall is usually taller, four to five feet high; combined with a high pitch roof, it can make the upstairs an actual "second story" with about three-quarters of the square footage of the floor below. Other walls need to be five to eight feet in height to become a full second story. Again, the difference is the pitch of the roof and the amount of space you desire.

The walls are erected much like those on the first floor of your log home. The problem is often getting them to the second level.

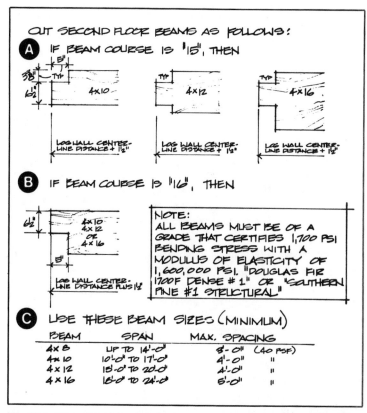

Fig. 12-3. Second floor beam selection and installation (courtesy Beaver Log Homes).

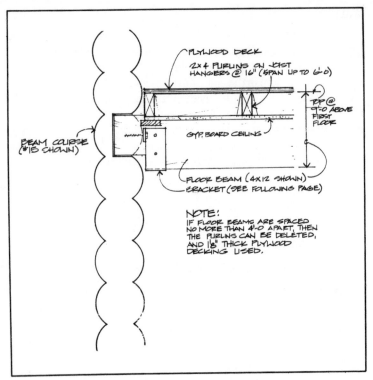

Fig. 12-4. Section through second floor framing condition in two story log wall (courtesy Beaver Log Homes).

This is solved with log ramps run from the ground to the second floor and pulleys to draw them into place. A sill plate is installed and logs are stacked, sealed, and spiked. Bucks are built for window and door openings if necessary.

The gable ends can now be brought to the second floor. If you're using a precut log kit, the gable ends are coded to identify the piece locations. If not, make sure that the dimensions across the gable ends of the building are the same as on your plans and that the gable structure is centered. Here are basic directions for erecting log gables included with a kit:

1. Start by laying the angle cut end logs of the gable row first. If an adjustment in length must be made in any row, do it on one of the logs in the center of each row, not on the angle-cut logs themselves.

2. Each row of logs should be laid up without caulking and spiking first to ensure the proper fit of that row. Then go back and install the caulking compound, spline, or seal strip and spikes. If you

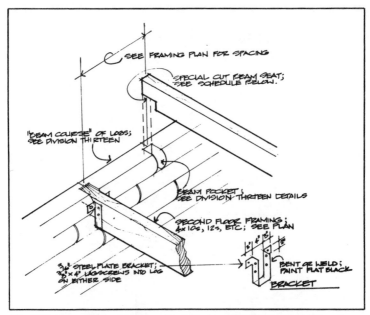

Fig. 12-5. Second floor framing schematic (courtesy Beaver Log Homes).

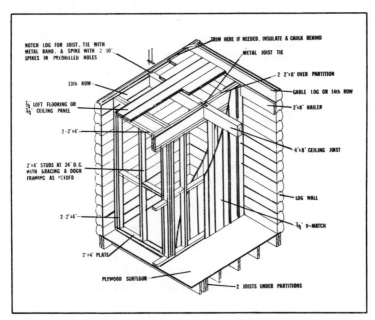

Fig. 12-6. Details of ceiling joists and partitions (courtesy Northern Products Log Homes, Inc.)

179

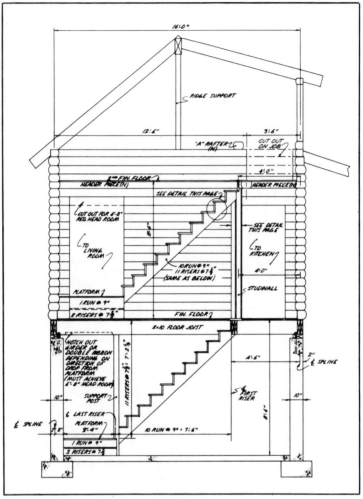

Fig. 12-7. Stair detail (courtesy New England Log Homes, Inc.).

have purlins in your plans, avoid spiking the gable logs in the area where you will later have to cut a purlin pocket.

3. Periodically check the gable to ensure that the center point of each row is lining up vertically with the center point of the wall below. You may want to establish a straight line up to the roof peak as a guide. This will prevent offset ridge points between two gable ends.

4. Complete the installation of the log, making sure you temporarily brace the gables as you go.

Rough log gables can be built similarly, making sure that each log placed goes beyond the sides of the gable. Then a circular saw can be used to trim the gable logs into a triangle to fit the roof's pitch and outline.

STAIRS

The second story is of little use without stairs, but the planning and building of a stairway can often frustrate the do-it-yourselfer. The first step is to determine the total rise of the stairs. That is, how far is it *vertically*—not diagonally—from the first floor to the second floor? That's the total *rise*. In most log homes it's between 7 feet 6 inches and 8 feet.

The next step is to figure the unit riser of the stairs. (The *tread* is the part you step on and the *riser* is the piece your toe kicks.) A flight of stairs has one more riser than it has treads; if you have 11 treads you will have 12 risers. Now divide the total rise (from above) by the number of risers; 7 feet 6 inches (90 inches) divided by 12 is 7½ inches per riser.

Then you figure the total *run* by multiplying the width of one tread by the number of treads. With a typical 10 inch tread, you multiply it by 11 in this case for a total run of 110 inches or 9 feet 2 inches. You may make the actual treads 10½ or 11 inches deep to allow for overlap of each step—called *nosing*.

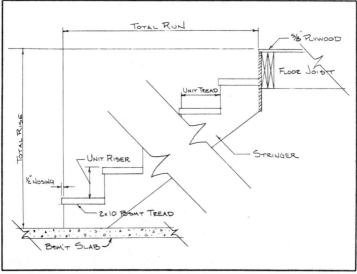

Fig. 12-8. Basement stairs (courtesy Northern Products Log Homes, Inc.).

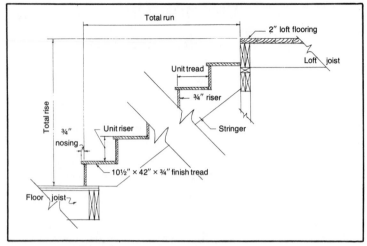

Fig. 12-9. Loft stairs (courtesy Northern Products Log Homes, Inc.).

Finally, the *stringer* is designed. Do it on paper first to save material and frustration. The stringer is log or timber that runs diagonally from the first to the second floor, holding the tread and risers in place. You can make it with dimensional lumber by cutting angles from a 2×12 board so that the treads and risers will be level. You can also use a log stringer by either cutting slots into the log for the treads—called *dado slots*—or by making the treads out of log slabs and supporting them with angle blocks.

One problem: As you remember, log walls compact. So build your stairs either on slides or hinges at the top or allow the final riser to "float," that is, don't nail the top of the stringer and final riser into the header plate at the top of the stairs. Otherwise, the compaction of the logs will bow the stairway.

UTILITIES

Utilities can be run to the second floor area in a number of ways. The most common is through interior frame walls. Plumbing, wiring, and even heating ducts can be installed between wall studs. If you're building with timbers you can make a central wall a hollow double wall. It helps to have upstairs utilities situated above first floor utilities: bath above bath, fireplaces above fireplaces, etc.

Others build a small utility closet that takes all utilities from one floor to the next. The advantage to this is that plumbing and wiring problems can be solved easier with centralized and accessible utilities.

Chapter 13

Installing Rafters and Trusses

Functionally, rafters, beams, plate, angle braces, and other components are designed and built to hold the walls in place while evenly distributing the weight of the roof. Without a well-engineered roof support system, your log home would soon look like Junior's log set the day after Christmas.

Aesthetically, the roof support members should complement the home's rustic design and blend into its mood. Your cathedral ceiling shouldn't be interrupted by a weathered and chalk-marked 2×4 jutting into the living room.

What seems to be a bad case of cross-purposes can become a functional and beautiful roof support system with a little planning and review. You can build a system that looks as good as it works.

PITCH

The first consideration in planning your roof support system is *pitch*, the slope of the roof. Your choice of pitch depends on local climate and internal space needs. A roof in snow country must have a greater pitch than one in the desert to allow for snow runoff. A home that requires the greatest amount of headroom on the second floor will also demand a steeper pitch to the roof.

Figuring the pitch is much like considering a stairway. The two facts you need are *rise* and *run*. The rise is the vertical distance from the top of the wall to the top of the roof. The run is the horizontal distance from the wall to the ridge. Pitch is expressed in the number

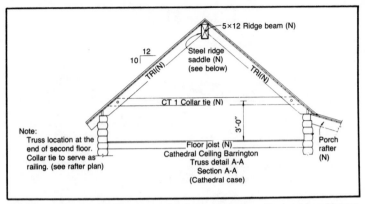

Fig. 13-1. Cathedral ceiling truss detail (courtesy New England Log Homes, Inc.).

of inches in rise for each 12 inches of run. That is, a 24 foot wide home with a central ridge that is eight feet above the wall has an "8-in-12" pitch—it rises eight inches in each 12 inches or run.

If you're buying a precut log home kit, the engineering department will tell you what minimum pitch you need for local conditions and space requirements. If you're building from rough logs, you can estimate the pitch of homes in your region or, preferably, have an architect or engineer design your truss system. There are many factors of stress-load that may only safely be planned by a professional who is familiar with both log construction and roof support systems.

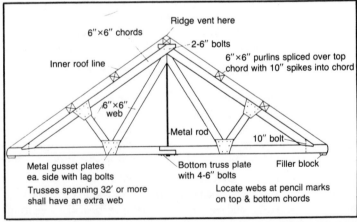

Fig. 13-2. Drawing of truss with 6×6 web support system (courtesy Northern Products Log Homes, Inc.).

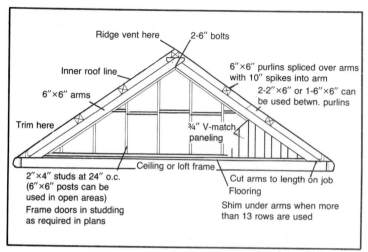

Fig. 13-3. Drawing of truss with arm set system (courtesy Northern Products Log Homes, Inc.).

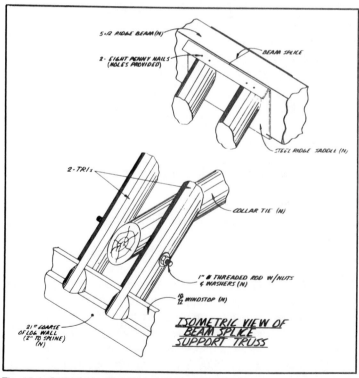

Fig. 13-4. Cathedral ceiling truss (courtesy New England Log Homes, Inc.).

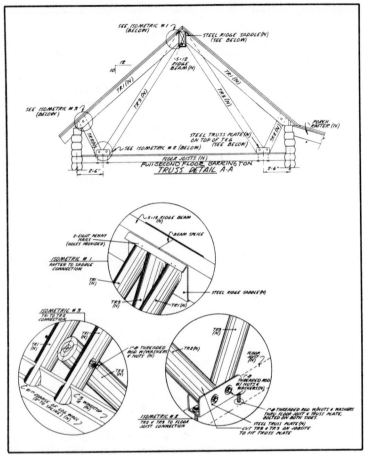

Fig. 13-5. Full second floor truss (courtesy New England Log Homes, Inc.).

BASIC ROOF SUPPORT SYSTEM

Let's take a look at the components and purposes of the roof support system piece by piece.

The *tie beam* is a large log, timber, or dimensional lumber member that spans the narrowest space between walls—usually parallel to the end gables. Its job is to hold the walls together and give support to central members of the roof system.

Rafters are the members that stretch from the top of the wall to the ridge of the roof. They are usually attached to the tie beam by *heel plates*, bolts, or metal brackets, and to the ridge beam with a *ridge plate*, bolts, or steel ridge saddle. Rafters also have an "extension" that extends out from the exterior wall to become the eave.

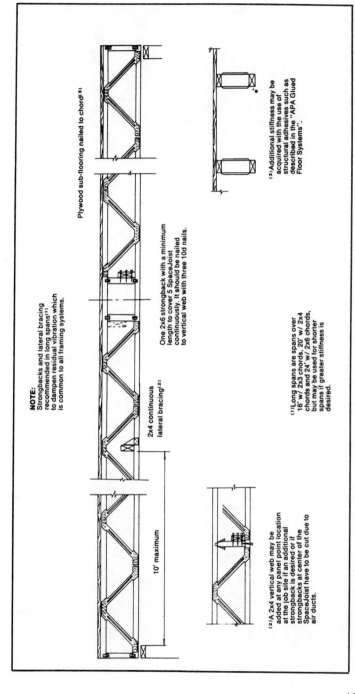

NOTE:
Strongbacks and lateral bracing recommended in long spans[1] to dampen residual vibration which is common to all framing systems.

Plywood sub-flooring nailed to chord[3]

2x4 continuous lateral bracing[2]

One 2x6 strongback with a minimum length to cover 5 SpaceJoist continuously. It should be nailed to vertical web with three 10d nails.

10' maximum

[1]Long spans are spans over 16' w/ 2x3 chords, 20' w/ 2x4 chords and 24' w/ 2x6 chords, but may be used for shorter spans if greater stiffness is desired.

[2]A 2x4 vertical web may be added at any panel point location at the job site if an additional strongback is desired or if strongbacks at center of the SpaceJoist have to be cut due to air ducts.

[3]Additional stiffness may be acquired with the use of structural adhesives such as described in the "APA Glued Floor Systems".

Fig. 13-6. SpaceJoist™ Bracing System (courtesy Lincoln Logs Ltd.).

Fig. 13-7. Brace walls into place before installing rafters and trusses (courtesy Lincoln Logs Ltd.).

The *ridge beam* is the highest member in the house and runs from one gable to another, tying the rafters together.

A simple roof support system may only contain these three members. A roof that has special angles or must support great weights will have additional members. The most common is the *center post* that runs vertically from the center of the tie beam to the underside of the ridge beam. It's tied into each with bolts or plates. Some systems will also have struts that run diagonally from the base of the center post to the center of the rafters on each side. This system is usually built with 6×6 or 6×8 timbers, but can be constructed with logs and patience.

A *purlin* is a member, usually a log, that spans from one gable to the other as horizontal support in the roof system. The horizontal purlin replaces the diagonally vertical rafter as the primary support. The purlins are tied to the tie beam with supports.

Fig. 13-8. Nail the other end of the brace to the subfloor (courtesy of Lincoln Logs Ltd.).

Fig. 13-9. Prebuilt trusses being moved into place for erection (courtesy Lincoln Logs Ltd.).

Roof support systems that are built in one large component are called *trusses*.

INSTALLING YOUR ROOF SUPPORT SYSTEM

If you're building your roof support system on the house from logs or timbers, here's how to do it:

First, notch the gable ends to receive the end of the ridge beams. Make sure that the notches are the same heights off the joist

Fig. 13-10. Trusses are ready to lift into place (courtesy Lincoln Logs Ltd.).

Fig. 13-11. A "crotch stick" is used to lift the truss (courtesy Lincoln Logs Ltd.).

course on both ends, or your ridge may be sloping to one end of the home and the rafters will be unevenly set.

Next, prop into place and spike or bolt the main rafters onto the ridge beam and wall plates. Then place and attach the other rafters in the system. Use scrap lumber to brace the gable and rafters together as you go.

Now install any center posts and struts as required, making sure that each piece fits tolerances on your blueprint. Also make sure that center-to-center spacing is correct and that members are level and plumb.

Fig. 13-12. A crew member climbs to the top of the wall to help position the truss (courtesy Lincoln Logs Ltd.).

Fig. 13-13. Trusses are attached to the top of the log walls (courtesy Lincoln Logs Ltd.).

Fig. 13-14. Trusses are tied together with stringers (courtesy Lincoln Logs Ltd.).

Fig. 13-15. Attaching the ridge beam (courtesy Northern Products Log Homes, Inc.).

Fig. 13-16. Purlins are nailed into position (courtesy Northern Products Log Homes, Inc.).

If you're installing purlins rather than rafters, notch the gable ends to support the purlin. Place the ridge purlin first, then install purlins in the center of each slope to hold the gables in place. Once all the purlins are in place you can add any supports between them and the tie beam.

If you're installing pre-built trusses made of dimensional lumber, the first job is to make sure that the gable ends are properly supported. Then hoist the first truss into place and, with a crotch stock, lift the ridge point into place. Next, install the ridge block and windstops between the gable and the truss as spacers. Check for

Fig. 13-17. The completed rafter and purlin system (courtesy Northeastern Log Homes).

Fig. 13-18. Positioning a log rafter on a one-story log home (courtesy New England Log Homes, Inc.).

Fig. 13-19. Drilling rafter tails for spikes (courtesy New England Log Homes, Inc.).

Fig. 13-20. Spiking down a no-tail rafter (courtesy New England Log Homes, Inc.).

Fig. 13-21. Rafters are nailed into the ridge beam (courtesy New England Log Homes, Inc.).

Fig. 13-22. House takes shape as rafter installation is completed (courtesy New England Log Homes, Inc.).

level and plumb, then raise the next truss and place it. Some trusses are tied together with a solid ridge beam that fit into a precut ridge notch in the truss.

Safety should be your first consideration when building your home. The fact is that more accidents happen during roof framing than in any other phase of construction. The larger materials combined with heights and incomplete components can multiply the risks. Inexperienced labor can further increase the chances of an accident. Be extra cautious and safety-minded during the installation of rafters and trusses in your log home.

Chapter 14

Roofing Your Log Home

Roof construction can be a pleasure or a pain. It's a pleasure to watch this part of log home construction go into place as quickly as it does. After spending weeks on building log walls, you'll enjoy seeing the roof take shape in an afternoon.

The pain can come from unforseen problems that stop construction right when the clouds begin building up in the east. It never fails.

The solution is to make sure you understand the steps of roofing your home and have planned everything out in advance of roofing day. In this chapter you'll learn about the what and how of sheathing, cutting required openings and building dormers as well as how to select, estimate, and apply common roofing materials. You'll also learn how and why many log home builders use double roof construction for function and beauty

SHEATHING YOUR ROOF

Sheathing is the wood covering placed over rafters or purlins that becomes the deck on which roofing materials are nailed. Local building codes may dictate the type of sheathing and roofing you use. The most common materials are 4×8 foot plywood sheets and 2×6 inch tongue-and-groove decking. Plywood is usually used where the bottom side won't be seen from below, such as over an attic or room with a ceiling. Tongue-and-groove decking is used where the lower side will be visible, as in a cathedral ceiling.

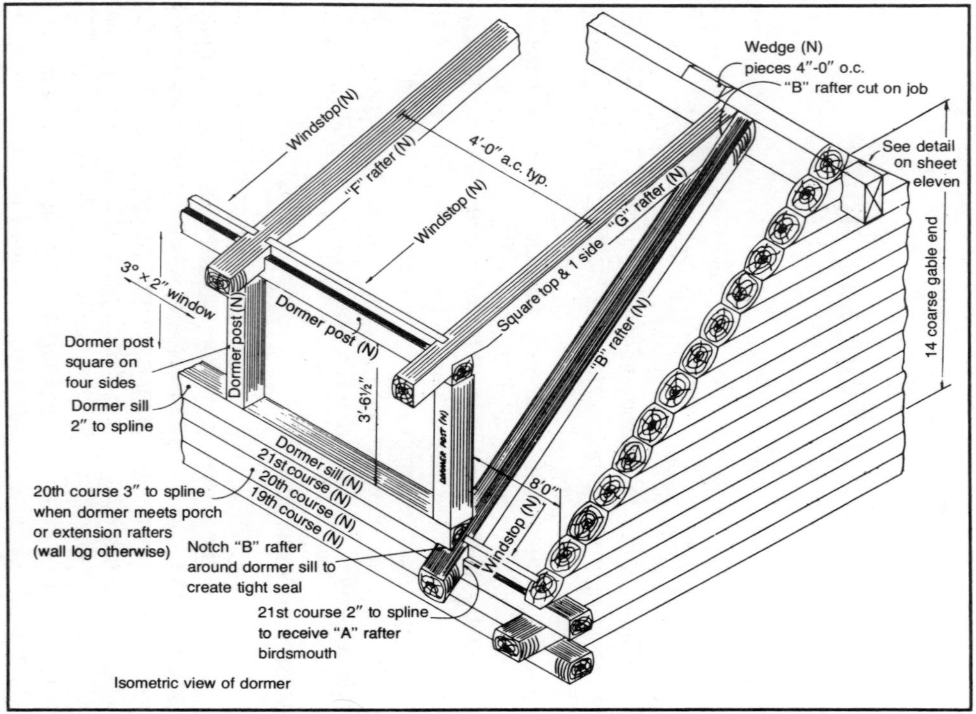

Fig. 14-1. Dormer construction detail (courtesy New England Log Homes, Inc.).

Labels within figure:

Wedge (N)
"B" rafter cut on job
pieces 4"-0" o.c.
See detail on sheet eleven
14 coarse gable end

DORMER POST (N)
"B" rafter (N)
"G" rafter (N)
Square top & 1 side
Windstop (N)
8'0"

"F" rafter (N)
4'-0" a.c. typ.
Windstop (N)
Dormer post (N)
3'-6½"
Windstop (N)
21st course (N)
20th course (N)
19th course (N)
Dormer sill (N)

Dormer post (N)
3°× 2" window
Dormer sill
2" to spline

Dormer post square on four sides

Dormer post 3" to spline when dormer meets porch or extension rafters (wall log otherwise)

20th course 3" to spline when dormer meets porch or extension rafters (wall log otherwise)

Notch "B" rafter around dormer sill to create tight seal

21st course 2" to spline to receive "A" rafter birdsmouth

Isometric view of dormer

198

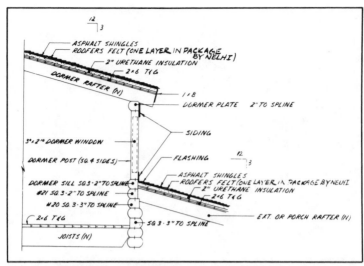

Fig. 14-2. Barrington dormer section (courtesy New England Log Homes, Inc.).

Fig. 14-3. Roofing begins with cutting and installing sheathing (courtesy New England Log Homes, Inc.).

Fig. 14-4. Preparation of windstop installation. Lower edge mating to windstop is splined, gasketed, and caulked. Windstop notches in rafters are caulked (courtesy New England Log Homes, Inc.).

Fig. 14-5. With the proper length of wind block cut, simply slide into place (courtesy New England Log Homes, Inc.).

Opening sheathing or decking is sometimes required by local codes under wood shakes. Open sheathing is simply horizontal boards with gaps between them to allow air to circulate from the attic to the shakes.

To install plywood sheathing, measure up 48 inches from the

Fig. 14-6. Applying caulking to upper surface of windstop and rafters (courtesy New England Log Homes, Inc.).

200

Fig. 14-7. Applying double strip of gasket to gable end surfaces (courtesy of New England Log Homes, Inc.).

upper edge of each gable end truss and snap a chalk line across all the trusses. Use this as a reference point for placing the first row of roof decking.

The decking must be well nailed to the trusses. Place nails 8 to 12 inches apart, except at the joints where they should be 4 to 6

Fig. 14-8. Installing roof sheathing (courtesy Northern Products Log Homes, Inc.).

Fig. 14-9. If skylights are used, assemble frame and cut hole in roof boards (courtesy Pan Abode Cedar Homes).

Fig. 14-10. Work progresses as decking goes up (courtesy New England Log Homes, Inc.).

Fig. 14-11. Bringing decking up the main roof section. This installation has interior chimney already built. Chimney can be built after roof is completed (courtesy New England Log Homes, Inc.).

Fig. 14-12. 2×6 decking being installed around chimney (courtesy New England Log Homes, Inc.).

inches apart. The joints should be staggered. Don't nail the first line of roof deck to the trusses until you have the second row in place. This allows you to move the truss slightly to make any necessary alignment adjustments. Be sure to sight along each truss for alignment before nailing down the decking.

Fig. 14-13. Cutting dressed edge for gable overhang (courtesy New England Log Homes, Inc.).

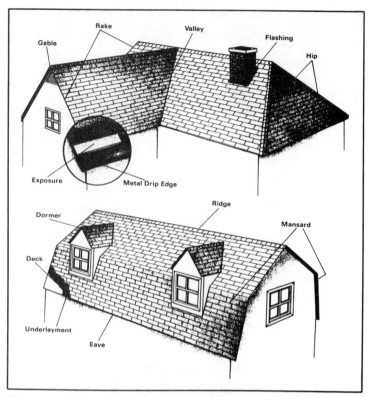

Fig. 14-14. Detail of roof construction (courtesy Lincoln Logs Ltd.).

If you're working with T&G roof decking material, begin laying it at the lower end of rafters. The first piece should have the groove down and the tongue up with the better side facing into the house. Allows at least a one foot overhang on gable ends. The decking may extend further randomly and later be trimmed off once you're done. If you're applying 2×6 T&G decking, use 20d galvanized nails and double-nail over each rafter and gable end.

Once all the sheathing is in place you can cut holes for vent pipes, chimneys, dormers, and skylights from below.

If your log home will have dormers on the second floor you can install them now. A *shed dormer* is simply one section of the roof that is lifted to a greater pitch and has a window installed in the end. A *gable dormer* will have its own ridge beam, rafters, gable, and sheathing. How it's built depends on materials you're using. It may be constructed from plywood, logs, or dimensional lumber. The steps are the same: frame it, add siding, roof it.

204

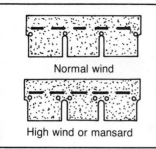

Normal wind

High wind or mansard

Fig. 14-15. Three-tab shingles (courtesy Lincoln Logs Ltd.).

ROOFING THE HOME

The most common roofing materials used in both frame and log home construction are asphalt shingles, wood shakes, and wood shingles. Asphalt shingles are the most popular—due to their lower cost—so let's cover them first.

The typical asphalt shingle is 12 inches high by 36 inches wide and has two slots in it separating it into three sections—called a three-tab. They come in bundles of a third of a *square*. A square is an area of roof which is 100 feet square. So three bundles will cover a 10 by 10 foot area of roof. To estimate the area of your roof, measure the dimensions of each plane on the roof including dormers. By multiplying the width times the length of each plane, you'll get the area in square feet. Add together the area of each plane and you have the total area of your roof. A roof that has two sides of 25 by 40 feet has 2000 square feet of roof area—20 squares, which will require 66 bundles of asphalt shingles.

You're also going to need *underlayment*, usually roofing felt or paper. This comes in rolls 36 inches wide and most rolls will cover four squares each. So for 20 squares of shingles you'll need five rolls of roofing felt.

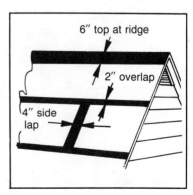

Fig. 14-16. Principal dimensions for laying roofing felt (courtesy Lincoln Logs Ltd.).

6" top at ridge

2" overlap

4" side lap

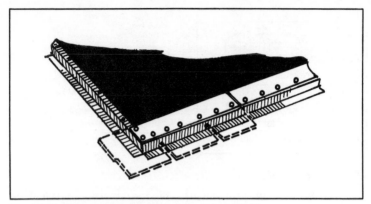

Fig. 14-17. Starter course (courtesy Lincoln Logs Ltd.).

Fig. 14-18. First course (courtesy Lincoln Logs Ltd.).

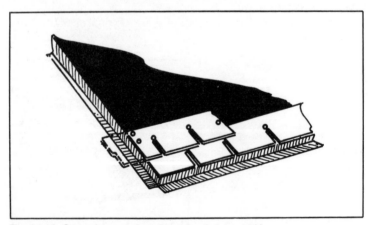

Fig. 14-19. Second course (courtesy Lincoln Logs Ltd.).

Fig. 14-20. Covering the completed decking with 15-pound builders' felt (courtesy New England Log Homes, Inc.).

How many nails? Most roofers recommend four nails per shingle which means about 320 nails per square. For 20 squares you'll need 6400 hot galvanized 11 or 12 gauge nails with ⅜ inch heads. Use half again as many nails on shingles in high-wind areas or on steep roofs.

Before you start, nail 8 inch galvanized drip edge around the perimeter of the roof, cutting with tin shears as necessary to fit. End joints should be butted, not overlapped. Nailing should be about 24 inch on center with galvanized shingle nails.

Next, apply aluminum valley flashing to any valleys in the roof. The bottom end of the flashing will have to be cut and formed to fit along the edges of the two intersecting roofs. Nail the valley flash-

Fig. 14-21. Overall view of shingling. From upper left to right: felt covered decking, layer of foam insulation, felt covering insulation, and shingles (courtesy New England Log Homes, Inc.).

Fig. 14-22. Bringing shingles up to the ridge (courtesy New England Log Homes, Inc.).

ing with shingle nails 12 inches on center and close to the edges of the flashing.

On a standard sloped roof (4-in-12 or greater), lay No. 15 asphalt saturated felt (roofing felt) horizontally with a 2 inch bottom overlap and 4 inch side overlap. The felt should overlap the ridge 6 inches. Now snap a chalk line over the felt horizontally every 10 inches.

The starter course uses trimmed shingles. Remove the tabs from enough shingles to go around the eaves of your house. Then cut 6 inches off the end of the first strip and nail it into place at the bottom left-hand corner of your roof. Use full 36 inch de-tabbed shingles across to the bottom right hand corner.

Fig. 14-23. Final courses (courtesy New England Log Homes, Inc.).

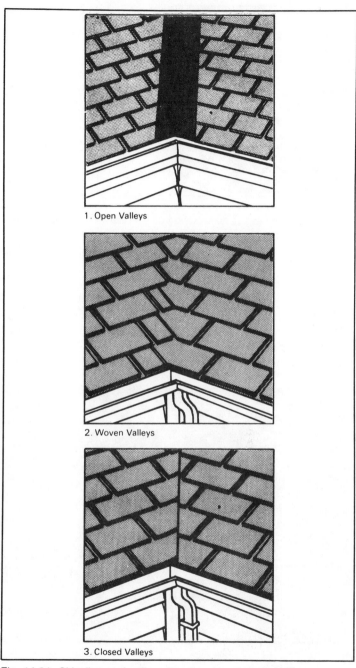

1. Open Valleys

2. Woven Valleys

3. Closed Valleys

Fig. 14-24. Shingling roof valleys (courtesy Lincoln Logs Ltd.).

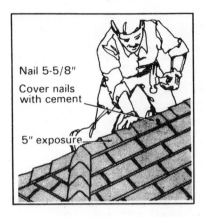

Nail 5-5/8"

Cover nails
with cement

5" exposure

Fig. 14-25. Installing hip and ridge shingles (courtesy Lincoln Logs Ltd.).

The first course is started and continued with whole shingles. In fact, every other course up the roof will begin with a full shingle. The second course uses a whole shingle with 6 inches trimmed off the left edge to offset the notch between tabs. Use the chalk lines as a guide to maintain parallel alignment with the eaves.

To cap off your roof job, close the intersection of the shingles at each ridge line with hip and ridge shingles. Cut three hip and ridge shingles from standard three-tab shingles at the cutouts and overlay them 5 inches on each side of the ridge. Nail them down with a nail on each side of the ridge under where the next shingle will lay.

Fig. 14-26. Final step is application of hip and ridge shingles (courtesy New England Log Homes, Inc.).

Fig. 14-27. Double roof construction (courtesy Northern Products Log Homes, Inc.).

In cold weather, always warm shingles before you bend them.

Metal flashing is applied around chimneys and vent holes as you lay the shingles.

Wood shakes can be made by hand with a tool called a *frow* and a mallet. All you need are a few 16 inch long cedar or redwood logs,

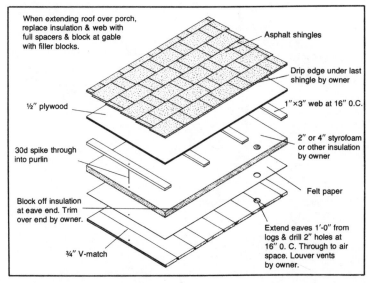

Fig. 14-28. Details of double roof construction (courtesy Northern Products Log Homes, Inc.).

these tools, and some time and patience. The log is stood on end and the frow (a wide cutting edge with a handle) is set on top of the log about ½ inch in from the edge. The mallet strikes the top of the frow to split the shake off the log just as you'd use a knife to cut a slice off a block of cheese. It takes time, but is both rewarding and inexpensive.

To apply 16 inch shakes, nail 1×3 boards horizontally between rafters as open sheathing. Space them about 7 inches apart all the way up the roof. Set the starter course so that the shakes overhang the eave or gable by about 2 inches and nail them into the 1×3 boards with two galvanized nails. The first course goes right over the starter course, staggering the gaps between the shakes. Start the second course with a half-width shake so that it overlaps the first course shake by 7 inches. Make sure that cracks between shakes are not above each other. Don't use roofing felt under your shakes. The idea is to let them breath as much as possible.

DOUBLE ROOF CONSTRUCTION

Some log walls won't meet local building codes for insulation factors—not because of their efficiency, but because of the R-factor

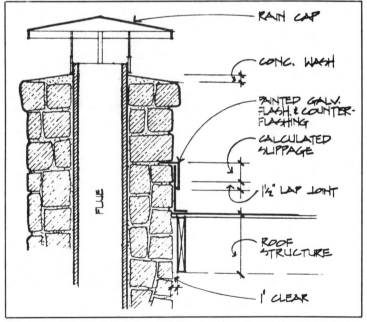

Fig. 14-29. "Slip-joint" flashing at roofline (courtesy Beaver Log Homes).

Fig. 14-30. Chimney flashing installation (courtesy Lincoln Logs Ltd.).

specifications. R-factors of other insulation are measured in zero percent humidity, an impossible figure for log walls that typically have 15 to 30 percent humidity. In any case, you may have to put additional insulation in the floor and roof of your log home to bring it up to the code. This is done with double roof construction.

Double roof construction is also used if you want to retain the look of tongue-and-groove ceilings while still having electrical, heating, and insulation materials in the ceiling. The T&G serves as the base of the double roof (the ceiling) and conventional roofing and sheathing is overlayed in a box sill arrangement.

Once the tongue-and-groove ceiling is placed, felt paper is laid over the entire roof just as you would if you were going to lay asphalt shingles. Then wiring is run over and through the roof as needed. Next, the insulation is put down—2 or 4 inch styrofoam or fiberglass packs. Then 1×3 boards are nailed down vertically every 16 inches, followed by plywood sheathing and asphalt shingles. This method is more expensive than conventional roofing, but can solve several problems at once.

Some log homes will have 1×10 boards installed on the gable ends of the roof (called *barge boards*) and 1×8s along the eaves (*fascia boards*) as final trim for the roof.

Your log home is finally enclosed. You've built the walls, installed windows and doors, possibly a second story, rafters, and roofing. You're ready to finish it off and begin living in it.

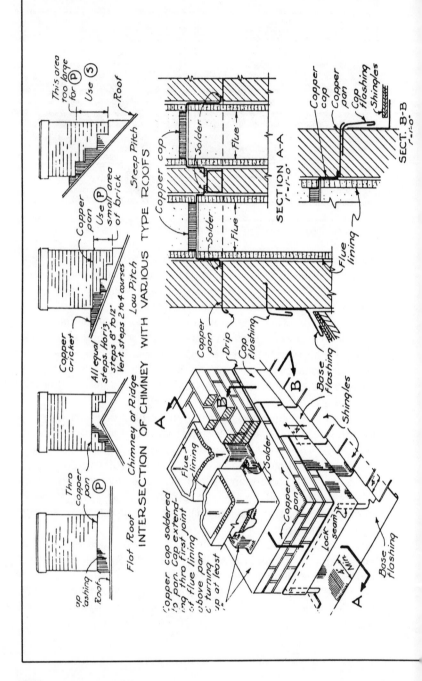

Thro copper pan Ⓟ

Flat Roof

Copper cricket

All equal steps. Horiz: steps 8" to 12". Vert: steps 2 to 4 courses

Chimney at Ridge   Low Pitch

Copper pan

Use Ⓟ small area of brick

This area too large for Ⓟ Use Ⓢ

Roof

Steep Pitch

INTERSECTION OF CHIMNEY WITH VARIOUS TYPE ROOFS

Copper cap

Solder — Flue

Copper cap

Solder — Flue

Flue lining

SECTION A-A
1"-1'-0"

Copper pan

Copper cap
Copper pan
Cap flashing
Shingles

SECT. B-B
1"-1'-0"

Copper cap soldered to pan. Cap extending thro first joint of flue lining above pan turning up at least ...

Flue lining

Solder

Copper pan

Drip

Cap flashing

Base flashing

Shingles

Base flashing

Lock seam

Min.

214

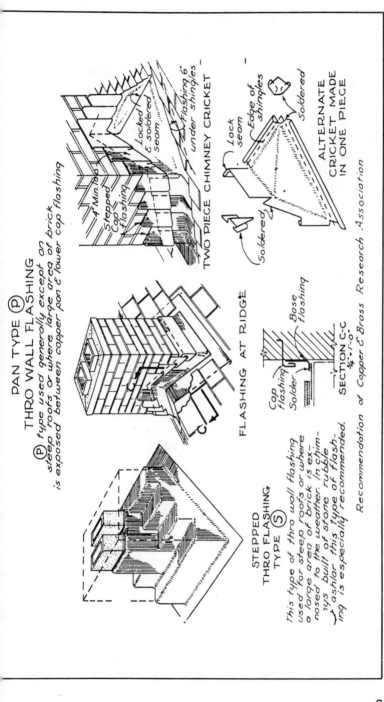

PAN TYPE (P)

THRO WALL FLASHING

(P) type used generally except on steep roofs or where large area of brick is exposed between copper pan & lower cap flashing

4" Min Lap

Stepped Cap Flashing

Locked & soldered seam

Flashing 6" under shingles

TWO PIECE CHIMNEY CRICKET

Lock seam

Edge of shingles

Soldered

ALTERNATE CRICKET MADE IN ONE PIECE

Soldered

FLASHING AT RIDGE

Cap flashing

Solder

Base flashing

SECTION C-C
⅜" = 1'-0"

STEPPED THRO FLASHING TYPE (S)

This type of thro wall flashing used for steep roofs or where a large area of brick is extended to the weather. In chimneys built of stone rubble ashlar this type of flashing is especially recommended.

Recommendation of Copper & Brass Research Association

Fig. 14-31. Roof flashing installation (courtesy Beaver Log Homes).

215

Chapter 15

Finishing Your Log Home

In a few weeks you'll be bringing furniture through the front door of your new log home to become its first occupants. You're naturally excited about the move and anxious to finish up.

However, careful planning and construction of the interior of your home can make a great deal of difference in your long-term satisfaction. After all, you'll be looking at the inside more than you will the outside.

Depending on your construction techniques and whether you're building from rough logs, a shell kit, or a complete log home package, the finishing stage goes something like this:

☐ Build interior walls.
☐ Install electrical and plumbing.
☐ Insulate.
☐ Cover interior walls.
☐ Install cabinets.
☐ Frame and mold doors and windows.
☐ Finish wood as needed.
☐ Cover floors.
☐ Install heating system.
☐ Finish hooking up utilities.

INTERIOR WALLS

Interior walls made from logs should either be built as you construct outside walls or, for non-loadbearing walls, can be added later. The addition is made by notching the ends of logs to butt the main wall logs and spiking them from the outside.

Most interior walls are built from dimensional lumber. The primary component is 2×4 studs. Here's how to build them:

First, locate the center lines of interior partitions and mark them on the subfloor with a chalk line. Center a 2×4 *shoe* or plate on the floor over the line, and nail it into place with 8d nails, 16 inches on center.

Then, using a straight 2×4, plumb overhead to locate the top partition plate and nail it into place with 8d nails, 16 inch center.

Find interior door openings and install jack studs and lintels—framing and header—according to your blueprints. The rough openings in stud walls should be framed out 2½ inches higher

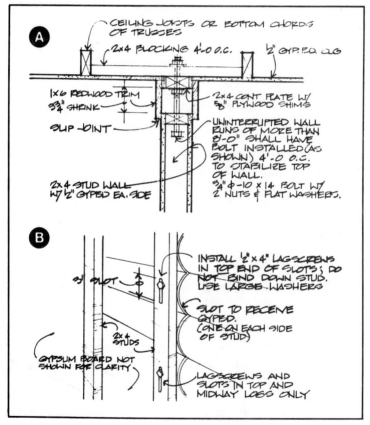

Fig. 15-1. Details of (top) interior partition construction and (bottom) interior partition attachment to log wall (courtesy Beaver Log Homes).

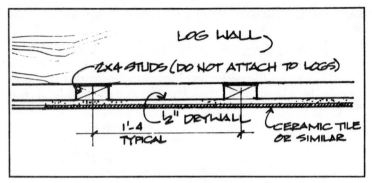

Fig. 15-2. Furred log wall for special finishes (courtesy Beaver Log Homes).

and wider than the door to allow for casing and shimming.

Install and plumb studs 16 inches on center between the shoe and top plate. Then cut and install horizontal blocking between studs according to the blueprint.

An alternative to building interior walls in place is to build them horizontally on the floor and raise them into place when complete.

We run into the problem of log settling again. As you've learned, the logs will settle with age and your home will probably be a few inches shorter within a year. What happens to interior walls when exterior walls shrink? Ready or not, they compact. The way to be ready is to build walls that can give. That's done by installing interior walls that are a few inches short and covering the gap between the top of the wall and the ceiling with a trim molding. Frame walls attached to exterior log walls must also allow for shrinkage with slotted studs.

WIRING AND PLUMBING

The wiring and plumbing schedules are usually developed by your electrician and plumber based on local codes and your requirements. While most of the work is performed in the conventional manner, a log building has special details that must be considered for smooth and efficient construction. If proper preparations are made, there's no reason for any wiring or plumbing to be exposed in your log home.

There are several guidelines for installing wiring in exterior log walls. Wall outlets are generally located two or three rows above the floor, depending on the desired height and code requirements. To do this, drill adequate sized holes down through the box headers to run your wiring. Mortices will have to be made in the log wall to accept the electrical boxes.

Another method of running wiring in the exterior log wall is to cut a notch or channel from the floor up along an exterior door rough buck so that wiring can be run behind the jamb trim. Then, at the desired height above the floor, drill a ½ inch diameter hole through the door buck at a slight angle to intersect with the mortise for the electrical box.

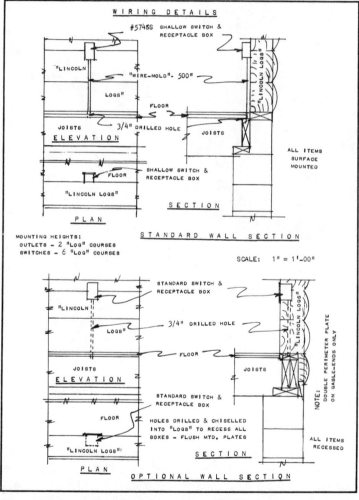

Fig. 15-3. Interior wall construction showing installation of electrical service (courtesy of Lincoln Logs Ltd.).

Fig. 15-4. Some wiring can be run through door and window jambs. Check local codes to see if conduit is required (courtesy Pan Abode Cedar Homes).

If you're building with beam ceilings, you may want to run wires to the ceiling fixtures in channels cut in the tops of the ceiling joists before they are installed. The channels can be made by a router or similar tool. This takes planning ahead. If lights are to be suspended from the purlins, the wires can be run between the first roof boards and second roof plywood.

Plumbing and electrical can be installed in framed interior walls just like in a conventional home.

INSULATION

To install fiberglass insulation between studs in frame walls you'll need a heavy-duty stapler, sharp knife, straight edge, gloves, and safety glasses. Use standard fiberglass batts or blankets with attached vapor barrier and of the correct width to fit between your stud pattern.

Kraft or foil-faced insulation should be installed with the facing towards the warm-in-winter side of the wall, rolling it out from the bottom to the top of the wall. Insulation scraps are used to fill in cracks around doors and headers above windows and doors. Faced insulation has a 1 inch stapling flange on both sides of the facing material. This may be stapled to wooden studs, joists, or furring strips by inset stapling. Push the insulation behind pipes and electrical boxes to help protect against pipe freezing and heat loss.

Friction-fit insulation has no vapor barrier attached. To install, simply wedge each batt in place between the studs. Then apply a separate vapor barrier such as 4 mil polyethylene film.

Fiberglass insulation can be installed in unfloored, unfinished attics by rolling batts of unfaced insulation out between joists. If foil-faced insulation is used, lay the vapor barrier down toward the warm-in-winter side.

Fig. 15-5. Interior plumbing wall (courtesy Pan Abode Cedar Homes).

Fig. 15-6. Interior wall finished with ¾ inch V-match pine lumber (courtesy Northern Products Log Homes, Inc.).

COVERING INTERIOR WALLS

There are a number of ways to cover interior walls, depending on your decorating ideas. Most log home owners prefer to decorate in colors and tones that enhance rather than detract from the wood finish of the logs. Browns are most popular. Walls can be finished in common plasterboard and painted or papered. Wood paneling can be installed, or planking can be used to cover interior walls and blend with the log-look.

Planking uses ¾ inch V-joint tongue-and-groove boards, either standard or random widths and lengths. It can be installed horizontally, vertically or diagonally, depending on tastes. Some kits come with this finish material.

INSTALLING CABINETS

Cabinets will be installed in the kitchen, baths and pantry area. Here's how:

First, set the base cabinets in place against the wall. On the top rail of the cabinet back, nail two finish nails through to the wall. These nails must be angled downward as steeply as possible to allow the timbers to settle. Do not use lag screws to attach base cabinets to the wall.

Next, upper cabinets should be attached to one timber only. Lag screws are permissible when installing upper cabinets. Since the upper cabinets will be moving downward as the wall settles, extra room must be left above the refrigerator. Typically, upper cabinets are installed with a 7 foot distance between floor and cabinet top. You may want to add 2 to 3 inches to this dimension to allow for settlement.

Finally, when installing countertops, remember than the backsplash must not be attached to the log wall. The backsplash should be an integral part of the countertop.

FRAMING AND MOLDING DOORS AND WINDOWS

Interior doors are installed next. Install the door frames to the desired height, cutting the bottom of the side jambs as necessary to accommodate the floor covering you plan to use. The side jambs should be fabricated by nailing through the head jamb with three 8d finish nails. The assembled frames are then fastened in the rough openings by shingle wedges used between the side jambs and the jack studs. One jamb is plumbed and leveled using four or five sets of shingle wedges for the height of the frame. Then two 8d finish nails are used at each wedge area, one driven so that the doorstop will cover it. The opposite side jamb is now fastened in place with shingle wedges and finish nails using the first jamb as a guide in keeping a uniform width. The stops should be temporarily nailed into place until the door has been hung.

Fig. 15-7. Finished interior wall (courtesy New England Log Homes, Inc.).

Table 15-1. Treating Log Wall Exteriors (courtesy Beaver Log Homes).

Mfg.	Type	Luster	Coats	Recommended Coverage	Application	Drying time		Mildew Resistant
						Dust free	Recoat	
Pratt & Lambert	Alkyd Nat/Stain	Flat-semi transparent	2	200 Sq. Ft. per gallon	Brush or Spray	½ hour	16 hrs	yes
Sherwin Williams	Alkyd base	Flat-semi transparent	2	150 Sq. Ft. per gallon	Brush or Spray	2 - 3 hours	18 hrs.	yes
Olympic	Oil base	Semi / transparent	2	150 Sq. Ft. per gallon	Brush or Spray	-	48 hrs.	yes
Cuprinol	Oil base	Semi / transparent	2	150 Sq. Ft. per gallon	Brush or Spray	4 hrs.	24 hrs.	yes
Cabot	Oil base	Semi / transparent	2	150 Sq. Ft. per gallon	Brush or Spray	-	72 hrs.	yes
Hydrozo	Oil base	Flat (clear)	2	80 - 120 Sq. Ft. / per gallon	Brush or Spray	-	24 hrs.	no

Next, cut and install the door trim to both sides of the interior door openings. Then hang the door, and adjust and permanently nail the stops. Install locksets, thumb latches, and other hardware.

Trim can also be added to interior side of windows.

FINISHING WOOD SURFACES

To remove imperfections, dirt, and water stains that have accumulated on the wall logs and timbers, you may want to sand all or part of your home. You can devote as much or as little time to sanding as you desire. At the very least you should sand the butt ends of logs and timbers to prevent splinters and scratches after you've moved into your home. The butt ends should be sanded with a belt sander using 80 grit sandpaper.

Wall surfaces can be resurfaced with a vibrating sander using 80 or 100 grit sandpaper. Always wear a dust mask when sanding.

Because unprotected wood exposed to the elements will begin to bleach out in just a few months, you may want to apply the exterior stain as soon as possible.

Interior walls can be stained with Danish oil, stain wax, or other finish depending on your tastes and the type of wood you've chosen. If necessary, use putty before you apply the stain, allowing 24 hours to dry.

COVERING FLOORS

Floors can be covered with carpet, linoleum, wood, or a combination of these. The most common floor covering in conventional homes today is carpet and this preference often carries over to log homes. However, remember that a quality linoleum, vinyl, or wood floor can be just as maintenance-free as carpet, and often cheaper to install.

The best way to choose carpet quality is by depth and density. Since the face yarns take the punishment, the thicker the tufts and the closer they are to each other, the better wear you can expect. Bend the carpet back to see how thick the pile is.

Vinyl and linoleum floors are chosen by purpose—beauty or wear or easy maintenance—depending on the use: hallway, kitchen, bath, or living room.

There are many types of wood floors, most of them of smaller pieces of wood inlaid together. Make sure the wood is a hardwood and that the stain will withstand wear and is easy to maintain. Stay away from patterns that have numerous cracks that can trap dirt. If it does, consider surfacing it with a resin that will give it a smooth finish and reduce maintenance and wear problems.

INSTALLING THE HEATING SYSTEM

You've chosen your heating system by now and it's just a matter of putting it into place and connecting any distribution ducts.

Fireplaces have a long tradition as the focal point of the home, and they seem very natural in a log home setting. They can be small or large, conventional, free-standing, hanging, air-circulating, water-circulating, faced with brick, stone or even wood, according to your individual preference.

With today's concern for saving energy, the fireplace has received a reputation among some as a great waster of heat with much

Fig. 15-8. Ready to move in (courtesy Beaver Log Homes).

of it going up the chimney. However, its aesthetic value, and use as a warm gathering place for the family, the fireplace will continue to be a popular though not always *primary* source of heat.

Building a brick or stone fireplace is a complete book in itself. However, here's an overview of the components and considerations of installing a masonry fireplace. Your fireplace is heavy and will require a concrete or stone footing under the house to help keep it level and distribute the weight. It should extend at least a foot below the frost line. It's easier to install the footing before you finish the home, but it can be done if you decide to add it later.

The *hearth* is the floor of the fireplace and should extend two feet out and a foot to each side of the actual fireplace for safety. Better fireplaces have an ash pit and door built under the fireplace that can be cleaned out from behind.

The wall of your fireplace will be at least 8 inches thick and lined with firebrick or a steel lining. Jambs and the lintel are the support for the sides and top of your fireplace opening.

Dampers are cast iron frames with a hinged lid that can be opened or closed to vary the size of the throat opening. Dampers increase the efficiency of your fireplace. Above the damper will be a smoke chamber or shelf to prevent downdrafts. The opening from here on up is called the *flue*.

With proper design and a few accessories you can make your fireplace both efficient and beautiful.

Wood stoves and furnaces have enjoyed renewed interest in the last few years and should be especially popular with those living in the country where wood is cheap or free. Wood furnaces typically heat circulating air or water that is distributed throughout your house by ducts. Wood stoves heat the air around them and depend on convection circulation.

Here's something to remember: Installing a fireplace, wood stove, or furnace next to a log wall can be a problem. *Under no circumstances* should the fireplace be grouted into the log wall. Grouting will stop the settlement process. The fireplace should be framed with a casing, nailing all framing in the fireplace opening only to the spline. This casing can be made from wood, metal, or a combination. Between masonry and logs you should install plywood, rigid insulation, or fiberboard as a backing. Masonry shouldn't be installed in or around the wooden members of the gable. In fact, if possible, build your fireplace and chimney inside the home and away from a log wall.

Other common heating systems include electric radiant heat

(ceiling cable, baseboard, and wall heaters), oil and gas furnaces, heat pumps (that store and equalize heat), and alternative energy sources such as solar, wind, and water power systems.

The greatest interest has been in solar power heating. There are two types, active and passive. Active uses equipment and devices to gather, use, and convert solar energy for power generation as well as heating. Passive solar energy harnesses the sun's warmth and stores it until needed through energy walls and floors within your home.

There are so many different types of heating systems and combinations that the serious log home builder should consider them well in advance of actual construction and use the services of energy experts in planning and building their log home.

HOOKING UP UTILITIES

Finally, you'll tie in your utilities: electricity, water, septic and others.

Connecting to water may simply mean having a meter and shutoff installed. Or you may need to run a final line to the pump house and well. Your concern is to get dependable and potable water to your home with adequate pressure.

You've probably already installed your septic system. Now it's simply a matter of hooking into it at the edge or under the foundation. Make sure that the leach field hasn't been damaged by heavy equipment during construction.

If you've been working with a building permit, the inspector will come out for "final inspection" and attach an Occupancy Permit to your power box cover. The power goes on and you're ready to move in.

You've come a long way. You planned and built some or all of your log home. You've become self-sufficient while extending your friendships. You've renewed the pioneer spirit with modern day technology.

You've conquered a personal frontier.

Chapter 16

Maintaining Your Log Home

Today's log homes are built to last. Unlike many of the frontier log homes of a century ago, modern homes are usually built on solidly engineered and constructed foundations for support and protection from ground moisture and insects. With proper maintenance, many of today's log homes will be standing a century from now.

But what is "proper maintenance?" It's preventing the enemies of wood—moisture and insects—from weakening the logs. It's also solving problems before they grow.

As is true with all materials, wood, unless properly and routinely protected, will degrade when exposed to the elements. Wood's greatest enemy is repeated wetting and drying. With moisture change comes the swelling and shrinking of the logs, giving a foothold to "dry rot" (more properly, wet rot). Fortunately, wood is highly resistant to action of the sun, oxygen, and most common air pollutants.

Unfortunately, most common stains, sealers, and coatings which repel moisture are susceptible to the action of the sun and air. As a result, these sealers must be renewed as they break down in order to provide continued moisture protection to the wood. The hulls of wood boats in constant contact with water have to be repainted only every few years, but the varnish on the "top sides" has to be renewed nearly every year because of the sun and air.

For log homes in most areas, a good quality penetrating sealer with a high water repellancy rating is recommended for application

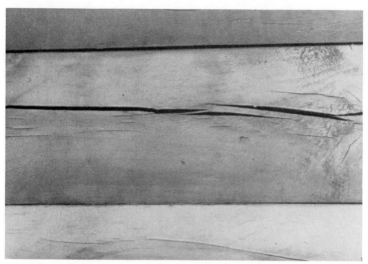

Fig. 16-1. Log checking and cracking (courtesy Northern Products Log Homes, Inc.).

during the home's first dry season. Soon after the wood has been sealed, caulking should be applied and then the building resealed. The frequency of the later resealings depend on the severity of the environment and the amount of sun (ultraviolet radiation). A dark color sealer will resist the sun much longer than a clear sealer, so some compromise between desired appearance and frequency of resealing must be made. When the sun breaks down the film of the sealer, moisture can enter. Clear sealers with high initial water

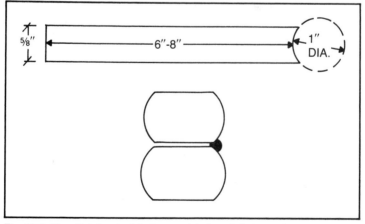

Fig. 16-2. Top. Pointing tool; bottom, pointed caulk between logs.

Table 16-1. Common Water-Repellent Preservatives (courtesy of Real Log Homes, Inc.).

Some Commercial Water-Repellent Preservatives Available
As Of September 1, 1980
For Exterior Wood Use Following Manufacturer's Directions And Cautions

Trade Name	Company	Address	Preservative Ingredient	Color
Woodlife	Roberts Consolidated Industries	600 N. Baldwin Park Rd. City of Industry, CA 91749	Pentachlorophenol	Clear and Brown
Woodtreat C81	Koppers Co., Inc.	Pittsburgh, PA 15219	Copper 8 Quinolinolate	Light Green
Cuprinol Stain & Wood Preservative	Darworth, Inc.	Tower Lane Avon, CT 06001	Tri-n-butyl-tin Oxide	Various
Cuprinol #20 Clear	Darworth, Inc.	Tower Lane Avon, CT 06001	Zinc Naphthenate	Clear
Penta-WR	Chapman Chemical Co.	Memphis, TN	Pentachlorophenol	Clear
CWF	The Flood Co.	Hudson, OH 44236	Pentachlorophenol	Gold-Brown
Pentaseal	Zehrung	2201 N. W. 20th Ave. Portland, OR 97209	Pentachlorophenol	Clear
Cabot Stains	Samuel Cabot, Inc.	One Union Street Boston, MA 02108	Various, primary Creosotes	Various
ZNS Wood Preservatives	Continental Products Co.	1150 East 222nd St. Euclid, OH 44117	Zinc Naphthenate	Clear
Wood Preserving Stains	OSMOSE Wood Preserving Co. of America, Inc.	980 Ellicott Street Buffalo, NY 14209	Tri-n-butyl-tin Oxide	Various
Clear Wood Preservative	Hydrozo Coatings Co.	855 W. Street Lincoln, NE 68501	Zinc Naphthenate	Clear
Cetol, Rubbol THB[2]	B.V. Sikkens	2170 BA Sassenheim, Holland	[1]	Various
Varapel	Flecto Co., Inc.	Flectco International Ltd. Oakland, CA 94608	[1]	Various

NOTE: Please contact your local paint distributor for the appropriate product in view of your intended use and local conditions.
[1]Fungicide added to protect coating. Not registered as a preservative.
[2]Available through Real Log Home dealers.

Fig. 16-3. Interior walls can be treated in many ways (courtesy New England Log Homes, Inc.).

repellancy (film) may have a short life. A pigmented sealer with less initial film may last a good deal longer and result in greater effective protection. The choice of the sealing agent should be made after talking with an experienced paint dealer who has lived in the area where the building is being built.

Fig. 16-4. Log home living room (courtesy New England Log Homes, Inc.).

Fig. 16-5. Interior frame wall is paneled and stained to blend with log wall (courtesy New England Log Homes, Inc.).

CHECKING AND SPLITTING

Checking and splitting in logs and larger dimensional timbers is common. It's the nature of material this size to shrink faster on the outside than on the inside, and this causes the checking and splitting of the wood. It doesn't mean that your house is going to fall apart or be structurally weakened in any way. Most woods only split to the "heart" of the log and not all the way through.

Fig. 16-6. Interior of completed timber wall home (courtesy Justus Homes).

One way to slow down this process is to use a humidifier in the house during the drying, winter-heating months of the year. This will add moisture to the air in the house and also be beneficial to the occupants of the house. However, the checking and splitting will occur as a normal process and is nothing to worry about.

CAULKING

All cracks—between logs and from splitting—should be caulked. The best caulking for any exterior application is one in which adhesion and cohesion factors are in balance, where elasticity and elastic recovery are greatest, and where there is the utmost resistance to ultraviolet radiation and oxidation. Acrylic rubber caulking is often chosen.

Before starting to caulk, make sure the logs are dry to the touch and above 40 degrees F. If there is an accumulation of sand or dust in the joints, blow them out with air or dust with a dry paint brush. Cut the nozzle on a 30 degree slant with about a 5/16 inch hole. Caulk with the gun leading the nozzle, but go slowly enough so the caulking slightly "billows up" behind the nozzle. Caulk about 12 feet—about half a tube—and then "point" the caulking.

Pointing is simply forcing the caulk into the wood fiber and smoothing the bead out with a small pointing tool you can make from

Fig. 16-7. Cathedral ceiling with exposed log beam and rafters (courtesy New England Log Homes, Inc.).

Fig. 16-8. Finished stairway to sleeping loft (courtesy New England Log Homes, Inc.).

a thin piece of wood by cutting a concave partial-circle on the end. You drag the pointing tool in the same manner the caulking gun is moved, at about a 45 degree angle to the wood. The tool should be positioned so that the center of the concave curve is maintained at the center of the seam or split. If the caulking does not extend to the edges of the tool when pointed, apply additional caulk and repoint. If you've applied too much caulking, caulk beyond the edge of the tool can be picked off with a knife immediately after pointing, or pulled off about 20 minutes after application.

Checks in the logs wider than 1/32 inch at the surface should be

Fig. 16-9. Open ceiling over kitchen and dining room (courtesy New England Log Homes, Inc.).

caulked, particularly if they are on the part of the log above the horizontal. A tube of caulking cut square at the nozzle with about a 3/16 inch hole is best. Hold the gun perpendicular to the log and force the caulking into the check. Let it billow up slightly behind the nozzle. Do not "point" checks. If a check or seam is wider than 3/16

Fig. 16-10. Finished log home bedroom (courtesy New England Log Homes, Inc.).

Fig. 16-11. The complete log home (courtesy New England Log Homes, Inc.).

inch and if it's deep, fill it first with fiberglass, rockwool, oakum, or paper to within ¼ inch of the surface before applying caulking.

Finally, a few don'ts: Don't caulk when the temperature is below 40 degrees. Don't caulk when it's wet. Don't caulk if it's raining or rain is threatening. If possible, don't caulk in the direct sun. Don't let caulk tubes or cartons sit in the sun.

About 30 days after caulking, a second coat of sealer should be applied to the building. When applying sealer it's a good idea to have a caulking gun handy to touch up any thin spots.

PROTECTING DOORS AND WINDOWS

Exterior doors and window sashes should be coated with urethane finish, paint, shellac, or boiled linseed oil. Apply several coats with special attention given to all edges, top and bottom of the door.

At least once a year, inspect all doors and windows for weathering and reseal any wood surfaces where moisture could enter the wood.

KEEPING INSECTS AWAY

You probably installed a termite shield on top of your foundation and below all wood surfaces to ensure that the little buggers couldn't easily infest your home. There are other things you can do to keep them out. First, keep dirt away from wood. Make sure that wood is at least 8 inches above the ground by keeping dirt low around the foundation. And dirt should be at least 18 inches below floor joists under your log home. Also, keep bushes and plants away from the side of your house. This year's small plants can become a ladder for termites and other borers within a few years.

If you're living in an area where bugs are a problem, talk with a local exterminator about a service contract. Most will treat your home in season with chemicals the consumer can't buy, and they often guarantee your home against bugs. But make sure you know what you're getting before you sign.

INTERIOR MAINTENANCE

You can brighten the inside of your log home with urethane or boiled linseed oil. However, before doing any finishing, test a small area at some obscure location of a log wall to make sure that you like the final results. If you're satisfied, the rest of the home can be done. When applying any paint or finish, don't smoke or have any open flame in the home. Keep doors and windows open so that vapors can be expelled. And make sure that logs have sufficiently dried before starting.

Many stains can be removed from interior log walls with a solution of oxalic acid and water. Oxalic acid can be purchased at drug stores and paint stores.

A century or two from now your descendants may be living in a log home that you built from rough logs or a kit. You will have left them not only a warm and efficient shelter, but also an insight into how people chose to live in the 1980s.

Appendix

Log Home Kit Manufacturers

These are the largest of approximately 200 log home kit manufacturers in the United States. A more complete and updated list of manufacturers in the U.S. and Canada appears in the *Log Home Guide* magazine published by Muir Publishing Co., Ltd., Gardenvale, Quebec, Canada H9X 1B0.

Air-Lock Log Company
P.O. Box 2506
Las Vegas, NM 87701

Alpine Log Homes, Inc.
Box 85
Victor, MT 59875

Alta Industries, Ltd.
Box 88, Route 30
Halcottsville, NY 12438

Arkansas Log Homes, Inc.
P.O. Box 959
Highway 71 South
Mena, AR 71953

Authentic Homes Corp.
Box 1288
Laramie, WY 82070

Beaver Log Homes
P.O. Box 1145
Claremore, OK 74017

(Additional factories in Blountstown, FL; Chadron, NE; Crosslake, MN; Malin, OR; and Spokane, WA)

Boyne Falls Log Homes
Highway 131
Boyne Falls, MI 49713

(Additional factory in Montana)

Building Logs, Inc. (Lok-Logs)
P.O. Box 300
Gunnison, CO 81230

Cabin Log Co. Of America
2809 Hwy 167 North
Lafayette, LA 70507

Carolina Log Buildings Inc.
P.O. Box 368
Fletcher, NC 28732

Green Mountain Cabins, Inc.
Box 190
Chester, VT 05143

Heritage Log Homes, Inc.
Box 610
Gatlinburg, TN 37738

Justus Company, Inc.
P.O. Box 98300
Tacoma, WA 98499

Lincoln Log Homes, Inc.
1908-A North Main
Kannapolis, NC 28081

Lincoln Logs Ltd.
Riverside Drive
Chestertown, NY 12817

Lodge Logs
3200 Gowen Road
Boise, ID 83705

Lok-N-Logs, Inc.
R.D. #2, Box 212
Sherburne, NY 13460

Lumber Enterprises, Inc.
Model Log Homes
75777 Gallatin Road
Bozeman, MT 59715

National Log Company
P.O. Box 68
Thompson Falls, MT 59873

New England Log Homes, Inc.   *(Additional factories in Mas-*
2301 State Street   *sachusetts, Virginia and Mis-*
Hamden, CT 06518   *souri)*

Northeastern Log Homes, Inc.
Kenduskeag, ME 04450

Northern Products Log Homes, Inc.
P.O. Box 616
Bangor, ME 04401

Pan Abode Cedar Homes
4350 Lake Washington Boulevard, North
Renton, WA 98055

Real Log Homes, Inc.
P.O. Box 8509
Missoula, MT 59807

Rocky Mountain Log Homes
3353 Highway 93 South
Hamilton, MT 59840

Rustic Log Homes, Inc.
1207 Grover Road
Kings Mountain, NC 28086

Rustics of Lindbergh Lake, Inc.
Condon, MT 59826

Sierra Log Homes, Inc.
P.O. Box 2083
Carson City, NV 89701

Traditional Living, Inc.
(Real Log Homes)
P.O. Box 202
Hartland, VT 05048

Traditional Log Homes, Inc.
P.O. Box 250
State Road, NC 28676

Vermont Log Buildings, Inc.
P.O. Box 202
Hartland, VT 05048

Ward Cabin Company
Box 72
Houlton, ME 04730

Wilderness Log Homes
Route 2
Plymouth, WI 53073

Glossary

air-dried lumber: Lumber which has been left to dry to a point where moisture content is in equilibrium with the temperature and relative humidity of the atmosphere.

anchor: Bolt, plate, rod, strip or other device used to secure one material to another. An anchor bolt is commonly ½ inch by 18 inches, used to secure the sill plate to the foundation wall.

backfill: Replacing soil into the excavated area around the outside of a foundation.

baseboard: A board (1×6 lumber) attached to the inside face of the square three logs of a log home. The wiring is placed behind this baseboard in a furred chase.

base molding: Molding used to trim the lower edge of the baseboard.

batten: Narrow strips of lumber used over the joints of the vertical siding or wallboard of a home. A board and batten combination is recommended finish material used on the dormer of a log home.

birdsmouth: The cut located near the end of tailed rafters. The birdsmouth cut rests on the top log courses.

bridging: Wood spacers inserted between the floor joist members on the first floor.

buck frames: Rough window and door frames made of 2×4 or 2×6 lumber and constructed on the job site.

butt joint: The point at which two logs meet in a log wall.

cathedral truss: Also called a *scissor truss*, these are prefabricated roof support sections with a steep interior ceiling pitch in lieu of the standard flat pitch.

checking: Cracking and splitting of wood due to drying process, common to large dimensional material.

chord: Either top or bottom chord, these are the top or bottom pieces or section of roof or floor trusses. Normal dimensions may be 2×4, 2×6, 2×8 or 2×10.

collar tie: The log which connects opposite walls in the cathedral ceiling section of the log home.

condensation: Water formed by warm, moist air contacting a cold surface.

conduit, electrical: A pipe in which the electrical wiring is installed.

course, log: All of the logs located at any particular height within the log wall, i.e., base course, second course, or "A" course, "B" course, etc., depending on the manufacturer.

crawl space: The space between the floor joists and the surface below when there is no basement. This area is used in making repairs on plumbing and other utilities.

crotch stick: A long piece of scrap lumber with a V notch in one end. It's used to lift trusses into place.

dormer: A projection from a sloping roof which gives more headroom in the second floor of the home. Windows can be installed in this dormer section.

double hung window: A window having top and bottom sashes, each capable of movement up and down.

drip cap: A metal or wood molding or flashing placed over a window or door to enable the water to run off the top of the unit.

drip edge: A metal molding designed to prevent the edge of the roof from leaking.

dunnage: Members used as a temporary foundation or base for stacking materials.

eaves: The projecting edge of a roof.

end groove: A vertical kerf, cut out of the center portion of a log wall. A piece of fiberglass spline must be inserted in this groove to provide a tight seal.

facia: A flat board used to cover the dormers or eaves of the roof.

facing: A covering layer for ornament or protection.

flashing: Sheet metal or builder's felt used to protect various parts of log homes from water seepage such as over the box sill and over the doors and windows, around chimneys, and at the intersections of roof planes.

footing: A concrete base wider than the foundation, used to support the vertical foundation wall, reinforced with #4 rebar.

foundation: The vertical structure which supports the first floor construction and which is partially located below grade level.

gable: The pitched portion of the home located above the eave section.

gable end: Normally the short end or side of your building.

gambrel: A roof having its slope broken by another angle.

gasket: The soft, pliable material used to seal the area between individual log courses. This material can expand or contract as conditions dictate. It's also used around windows and door jambs.

girder: The large horizontal structural member usually heavier than a beam used to support the ends of joists and beams.

grout: A liquid sealer which is used to fill in joints and cavities of any concrete or masonry work. It's also used under a sill to provide a flat bearing surface.

header: A beam used as a connection between joists and rafters. The purpose of the header is to allow room for a fireplace, stairway, window or door.

hip: The external angle formed where the two sloping sides of a roof meet.

hip & ridge: The shingle material which forms a tight seal over the hip and ridge portion of the roof.

jamb: The side, head and sill lining of any window, door or other opening.

joist: The structural members which support the floor and ceiling loads. In many kits, the first floor joists are 2×10s and the second floor joists are 12 to 16 foot long logs.

kiln-dried: Material which has been dried by artificial means. Lumber which has been kiln-dried will have a moisture content of approximately 19 percent when it leaves the kiln.

lally: A concrete filled pipe used for support.

lally column: A post that supports a beam or timber.

lateral bracing: 2×4 bracing run across the bottom chord of either roof or floor trusses, to support and minimize the twisting of the trusses.

loadbearing wall: A wall that supports its weight as well as that located above it.

lumber: Material less than two inches thick and more than two inches wide are called *boards* or *board lumber* while material from two to five inches thick and two or more inches wide is called *dimensional lumber*.

mortise: A slot cut into a wall log to facilitate the joining of corners.

non-bearing wall: A wall which supports only its own weight.

no-tail rafter: A rafter which has no portion of its length overhanging the log wall on the outside. It has no "birdsmouth" cut.

on center (O.C.): The usual measurement for spacing studs, rafters, floor joists and other members. It's the measurement from the center of one member to the center of the next.

penny (d): The length of a nail. It originally referred to the price of 100 of a certain size nail. Today it has no bearing on the cost of the nail, but is still used to refer to sizes: *6d* or *six penny nail*.

pier: A column of masonry used to support other members of a home such as the porch sills.

pitch: A term applied to the amount of roof slope. It's found by dividing the height by the span. A pitch of six means that the roof projects up six inches for every 12 inches of horizontal run.

plate: A horizontal member which supports other members: sill plate, dormer plate, etc.

plumb: A member or unit which is exactly vertical, or the quality of being exactly vertical.

plumb cut: The cut at the end of a rafter which butts up against the ridge board or windstop.

plywood: Wood sheathing made up of three or more layers of veneer bonded with glue.

poured concrete: A foundation constructed of concrete poured into frames versus concrete block construction.

preservative: A compound, applied as a liquid, which is used to prevent rot or insect damage to wood.

purlin: Beam material used in roof framing.

rafter: A structural member used to support the roof, running from the eave to the ridge. The roofing is nailed directly to the top of the rafters.

ridge: The top junction of two sloping surfaces, such as a roof ridge.

ridge beam: The beam placed at the top of the main section of the house. The main roof rafters are nailed into this ridge beam. The ends of the ridge board can be inserted into the gable ends.

ridge vent: Sections of metal venting installed along the peak of the roof and used to provide ventilation in the attic.

riser: The vertical material used to span the space between stair treads.

rough openings: Rough dimensions needed for window and door installation. The rough opening for a window is the inside dimension of the appropriate buck frame.

sash: A single frame containing one or more lights of glass. A window is generally composed of two sashes.

scaffolding: An assembly used to reach higher elevations during construction.

shake: A thick, handsplit wood shingle.

sheathing: The covering placed over studs or rafters of a home, usually plywood or boards.

shingles: The roof covering of a home. They can be made of a variety of materials (wood, asphalt, clay, etc.), and come in various sizes.

sill: The bottommost member of a structure. The floor joists or studs rest on a sill.

sill plate: Usually a 2×6 pressured treated lumber used to set the first course of logs on the foundation.

skirt: A single row or course of log siding used to blend the first course of logs to the boxed or raised floor system.

slab: A poured concrete pad on which a building is constructed. Normally used in lieu of either a crawl space or full foundation.

snow blocks: Lumber used to block air and weather passable through the spaces between each truss and the point where they rest on the log walls.

soffit: The undersurface of roof eave or rake.

solid bridging: A solid member located between two floor joists near the center of the span. This prevents twisting of the joists.

spline: A strip of fiberboard which fits in the spline groove of two logs, one log above and one below. This provides a tight seal when coupled with the gasket.

square: A unit of measure for shingles which covers 100 square feet.

stack and vent pipe: A vertical pipe in a plumbing system used for ventilation and pressure relief.

staging: A frame assembly used to reach the higher elevations of a home during the construction phase.

strut: Bracing member of a truss.

stud: A vertical member placed in walls and partitions to form the basis of a wall.

subfloor: The boards or plyscore which is nailed to the floor joists and is used to affix the finish flooring.

tenon: A cut made to the end of a timber so that it will fit into the mortise of another timber or log, creating a tight fit and providing structural support.

termite shield: A metal shield placed over the foundation and other parts of the home to prevent termites from gaining access to logs and other wood.

tie: A framing member between rafters used to form a truss.

toe-nailing: Driving a nail at an angle through one wood member to another.

truss: A braced framework capable of spanning greater distances than the individual components; prefabricated roof or floor support sections.

valley: The trough formed by the intersection of two roof slopes.

vapor barrier: A thin sheet of plastic used to prevent the passage of water vapor.

wall bracing: Lumber used on the interior and exterior sides of the walls during construction to reduce the "rolling" of logs until the roof is complete.

windstop: Horizontal boards which fit between individual rafters and vertical between the roof and top log of the log home to provide a weather-tight seal at the eaves of the roof. Also called *snow blocks*.

Index